D0085451

# New Product Development and Marketing

# New Product Development and Marketing

## A Practical Guide

*Italo S. Servi*

New York
Westport, Connecticut
London

**Library of Congress Cataloging-in-Publication Data**

Servi, Italo S.
    New product development and marketing : a practical guide / Italo S. Servi.
      p.    cm.
    Includes bibliographical references.
    ISBN 0-275-93403-9 (alk. paper)
    1. New products—Management. 2. New products—Marketing.
3. Design, Industrial. 4. Intellectual property. I. Title.
HF5415.153.S47   1990
658.5'75—dc20        89-70956

Library of Congress Catalog Card Number: 89-70956
ISBN: 0-275-93403-9

First published in 1990

Praeger Publishers, One Madison Avenue, New York, NY 10010
An imprint of Greenwood Publishing Group, Inc.

Printed in the United States of America

The paper used in this book complies with the Permanent
Paper Standard issued by the National Information Standards
Organization (Z39.48–1984).

10  9  8  7  6  5  4  3  2  1

# Contents

# Figures and Tables

## Figures

## Tables

# Preface

Necessity and ingenuity were instrumental in the development of new products since primeval times, but initially progress was slow. Progress accelerated markedly during the industrial revolution and product complexity increased. In recent times, new product development became a very sophisticated process yielding countless innovations every day.

Does contemporary product development differ fundamentally from the caveman's search for a more efficient tool or weapon? Is man's ingenuity less valuable because of the availability of multidisciplinary teams and sophisticated equipment? Are teams becoming too complex and possibly unmanageable? What foundations have changed, over the centuries, and what foundations have remained invariant?

This book answers these and other questions by searching for commonalities and simplicity in the diverse and utterly complex field of Technology Management. It demonstrates how a few basic principles rule new product development irrespective of environmental factors, business goals, and level of effort. It guides the practitioners, so that they can raise the historically low batting average of technically and commercially successful new products, but allows no illusion that a methodology, a formula, or a technique can constitute a miraculous panacea.

Whereas commonalities are emphasized throughout, differences are also highlighted. Practitioners in various business segments can select the elements of the new product development process that are critical in their own environments.

The new product development process should follow the sequence indicated by the four questions of Figure P.1—WHY?, WHAT?, HOW?, and WHO? A fifth question—WHEN?—is pervasive. The developer must *always* be time sensitive. Success depends on being in the right place at the right time. Being too early or too late may lead to failures. Moreover, time is a commodity that cannot be generated, purchased, or borrowed and, when it is gone, it will never come back.

The organization of this book is consistent with the question sequence of Figure P.1. In Part I (WHY?), a product is framed within the company's prod-

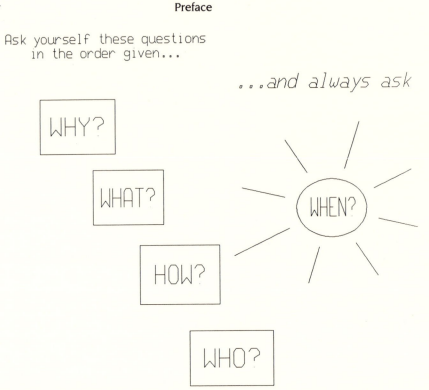

Figure P.1  The Five Questions of New Product Development

uct portfolio and within the engineered system in which it functions. Planning and planning methods are discussed briefly. The profit is emphasized, and other financial considerations raised.

In part II (WHAT?), a product is defined in the context of the market it attempts to serve. Sources of new product ideas and methods for ranking such ideas are described. Marketing research is discussed.

In Part III (HOW?), you will see how an idea or market need is converted into an article of commerce. This section addresses both the technical and the commercial aspects of new product development.

In Part IV (WHO?), the focal point is the all important human element. We shall talk about organization and communication.

This book ends with three outstanding examples of new product development and with a concluding chapter that synthesizes ways of increasing success probability.

This book is written *by a practitioner for practitioners*. It draws principally from my experience in industrial research, consulting, and teaching. I value theories and methodologies proposed since the dawn of the industrial research era; at the same time, I should stress the importance of individual judgment and intuition.

The limited bibliography highlights only a few of the many outstanding books and articles that have been written on product development and related subjects. There are many giants who have contributed to the clarification and rationalization of this very complex field of Technology Management. References to all their work is beyond the scope of this book and will not be included.

It is usually possible to select specific cases that support specific principles, while ignoring others that could refute them. Therefore, I do not analyze examples for the purpose of proving the validity of principles. Rather, I will give examples to clarify principal statements and reinforce concepts. They are drawn from history as well as from fictitious situations.

References to commercial service organizations and their products do not imply the author's endorsement or his lack of endorsement of alternative services that the reader may want to select.

I am indebted to the many organizations and individuals who contributed valuable information and documents. I want to express my special appreciation to Nancy Richmond Winsten for editing my first draft and making valuable suggestions on the organization of this book; to Charles River Associates, Inc. for assisting with the preparation of illustrations; and to Northeastern University for permission to use material from the continuing education course that I taught there.

## PART I

# WHY?—PLANNING

# 1

## New Product Planning

### Introduction

New product development is a *process* which starts from a motivating goal, moves through an idea conception phase, is reduced to practice in its implementation phase, and is completed in a transitional phase, during which the product becomes established.

To understand this process, we must first become aware of the different connotations of these three words: *new*, *product*, and *development*.

The advertising of many consumer products has praised new and improved articles of commerce which may be differentiated from older products based on minimal differences, such as a more attractive packaging. Are these really new products? Yes, as long as the manufacturer has, somehow, succeeded in increasing their market appeal. Likewise, clones are new products because they are affordable in new market niches.

The *legal* definition of new is not related to market appeal. According to the U.S. patent system, the novelty of a product is based not only on documented differences between it and prior art, but also because those skilled in the art cannot anticipate such product. Countless legally new products never become articles of commerce.

A product can be new to the market, or new only to a particular producer. It could also be an old product offered to a new market after appropriate adaptation. Most new products have a forerunner which may be technically similar, or merely fulfill similar functions. The abacus is a forerunner of the electronic calculator, and the buggy whip could be called, somewhat facetiously, the forerunner of the automobile accelerator.

The meaning of *new* is subjective, and often depends on the business that each enterprise practiced in the past.

Most principles discussed here apply to all kinds of products: an engineered system, a hybrid rose, an insurance plan, or a software package. The major emphasis in this book is on manufactured goods, and primarily on industrial products. While principles are similar for most product types, the most appropriate practices are likely to differ substantially, not only because of the nature of each product line but also because of the environment.

Products can be classified into three categories according to their users—consumer, industrial, and defense.

*Consumer products* are delivered to the ultimate users and eventually die there. Therefore, market needs can be defined by directly assessing the sentiments of those who will use the products for their own benefit.

*Industrial products* present more complexity because they are not purchased by the ultimate end users. They are used by a manufacturing concern to make other products. In the case of complex engineered systems, the time from the sale of a component to the operation of the entire system may be long (even several years). Thus large quantities of components may have to be marketed before receiving a significant feedback on their performance under system operational conditions. Usually, the farther the product is positioned with respect to the ultimate user, the higher the business risk.

*Defense products* can be regarded as either consumer or industrial. They are classified separately from the others because their procurement mechanics are singular, and because their performance is often based on unique criteria.

Development is both technical and commercial. Both are essential to bring a new product to fruition, and both should occur simultaneously, rather than sequentially, albeit with different intensity.

Before embarking on the description of the new product development process, its essential elements, problems, and their solutions, let us state a universal definition of successful new product development:

Successful new product development is the process that satisfies current or anticipated market needs by an intimate combination of technical and commercial endeavors, consistent with the business objectives of the developer.

## Product Integration Flowsheet

Most manufactured products that satisfy the needs of the ultimate users should be viewed as *engineered material systems*, in order to gain a broader perspective. An automobile, a computer, even a knife, a granular fertilizer, or a box of corn flakes is an engineered material system. One can then describe a material integration flowsheet, which starts from something coming from earth's ground, waters, or atmosphere, and goes through several processing steps (chemical engineers call them unit operations). Figure 1.1 gives a simplified representation of a generalized material integration flowsheet. Figure 1.2 gives a partial example of a personal computer flowsheet.

The makers of most products have the opportunity to make, rather than buy, some of the products they need in their operations. This is called backward integration. They have the opportunity to make products that their customers produce (forward integration), and could also manufacture other products that their customers need to build the material system (horizontal

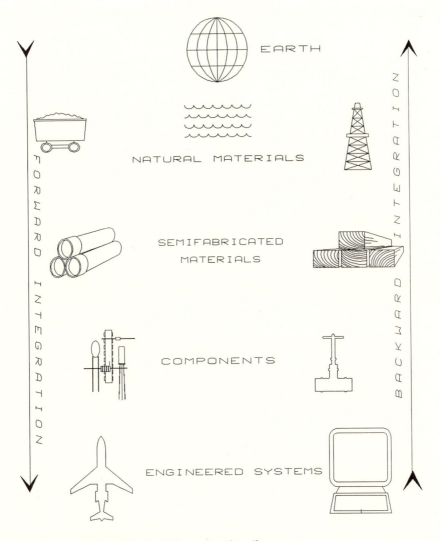

Figure 1.1  Generalized Product Integration Flow Sheet

integration). The maker of a hybrid circuit used in a computer (see Figure 1.2) can, for instance, integrate backwardly by manufacturing the circuit board and integrate horizontally by producing disk drives.

Most engineered systems, when sold and operated, also require consumable products and services, and generate disposal problems. Additional business opportunities derive from consumables, services, and disposal.

Viewing an individual product as a part of an operating engineered material system can, therefore, generate many ideas concerning new products that respond to market needs.

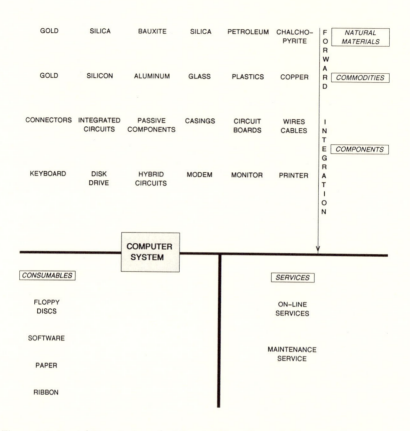

Figure 1.2  Partial Description of a Material Flow Sheet of a Personal Computer

Some additional products (consumables and services) are also indicated.

## Planning

New product development rests on three pillars: planning, technical development, and marketing. The focus of this section will be on planning.

In his terse and penetrating book,[1] Wallenstein distinguishes between destiny, functional, and interfunctional planning, and emphasizes the *interfunctional nature* of product planning. An awesome conclusion indeed, if we believe in Confucius' famous adage: "Those whose ways are different cannot do planning together."

*Destiny planning* concerns the overall guidance of an establishment and is the sole prerogative of the chief executive officer and his supporting staff. Destiny planning answers the ultimate WHY? question of the new product development sequence.

*Functional planning* draws the detailed roadmaps for operations, marketing, financial, and other sectors. It establishes procedural rules, standards, and assessment methodologies. Accountabilities for functional planning rest with each sector manager.

*Product planning* can neither be carried out by the chief executive officer (except in the case of very small, entrepreneurial companies where such officer, in effect, also performs the duties of several functional sector managers), nor by any one sector manager. Product planning must be *interfunctional* in order to be effective. The failure of many new products can be traced to the lack of such interfunctional planning, and the probability of such a failure is higher relative to the complexity of the organization. The success of small entrepreneurial companies has been historically superior to that of complex organizations because of the ease of interfunctional planning in such environment.

## The Product Portfolio

New products should always be planned after considering the entire product portfolio of the company. Such portfolio should include commercialized, embryonic, and developmental products.

One way of graphically representing a product portfolio, as defined above, is to adopt and modify the scheme (first suggested by the General Electric Company), whereby each product is judged based on its business attractiveness and company strength. We shall not be unduly concerned, for the time being, with the definition of the terms business attractiveness and company strength. We only note that these terms are, to a great extent, subjective, changeable, and difficult to quantify precisely.

The commercial products are plotted in Figure 1.3 as circles, whose surfaces are proportional to their sales volumes; developmental products are plotted as triangles of uniform sizes. Figure 1.3 represents the product portfolio map of a company at a certain point in time.

The initial product portfolio (Figure 1.3) indicates that most sales derive from the mature Product 1. The balance of the sales is divided between Product 2, which has excellent business potential and is in the area of company strength, and Product 3, which is, in all respects, unappealing. The two developmental products, A and B, are unfavorably positioned with regard to either business attractiveness or company strength. The company obviously needs to revitalize its product portfolio.

In Figures 1.4 and 1.5 we have developed two alternative scenarios that represent the product portfolio after a span of time—say, two years. The first portfolio is undesirable, the second desirable.

In the scenario exemplified in Figure 1.4, the company has commercialized both developmental products (now identified as 4 and 5), and maintained the other three products. The business attractiveness of the principal product (1) has decreased, with attendant deterioration of profit margins. Products 3 and 5 are in the area of company weakness. Products 2 and 4 require substantial

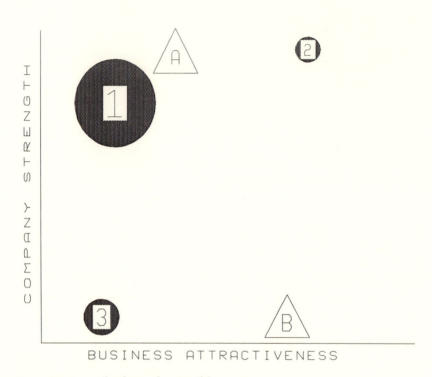

BUSINESS ATTRACTIVENESS

Figure 1.3  Example of a Product Portfolio

Circles indicate commercial products; triangles, developmental products.

resources in order to grow significantly. There are no developmental products in the portfolio, because most technical resources have been utilized to support the recently commercialized products. This company is heading for disaster!

In the scenario exemplified in Figure 1.5, the company succeeded in gaining markets for the very attractive Product 2, commercialized the developmental Product A (now called Product 4), which is in the area of company strength and reasonably attractive with respect to business, dropped the other developmental product, discontinued the former commercial Product 3, and initiated the development of a reasonably well positioned new Product C. This product portfolio is now sound, and the company is headed for business success.

The two scenarios are simplistic, because they do not fully consider the dynamic and flexible nature of the new product development process. Neither company strength nor business attractiveness are unchangeable over time. Company strength can be increased deliberately by appropriate staffing, by joint venturing, or by acquiring another operation. Business attractiveness can

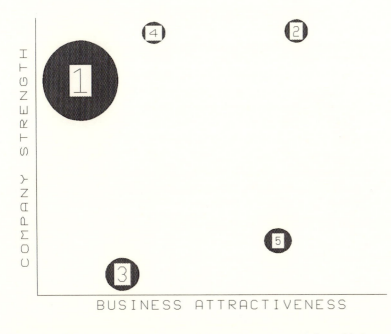

Figure 1.4  Product Portfolio of Figure 1.3 Two Years Later: Unfavorable Scenario

Figure 1.5  Product Portfolio of Figure 1.3 Two Years Later: Favorable Scenario

abruptly change in a favorable or an unfavorable direction because of unforeseeable external events.

Can company strength and business attractiveness be better defined and quantified? Undoubtedly so—after considering several factors. In the first case, technical resources, marketing capability, customer structure, geographical presence, and institutional stature must be considered; in the second case, growth potential, profit margins, and competition. One could rate these and other factors based on an arbitrary scale (the so-called figure of merit), attribute to each factor a different importance (the so-called weighing factor), and derive an overall rating figure by multiplying these two indices. Sole dependence on such mechanistic approach is not desirable, but this methodology becomes viable when it is somewhat tempered by qualitative and intuitive judgment.

## Examples

These examples illustrate and clarify some of the concepts, principles, and issues previously enunciated. They describe three successful new product development planning schemes.

### Metal Commodities

Metalcom, Inc. (a fictitious name) is a major producer of a metal commodity (such as nickel, chromium, or molybdenum). Its product is fungible; that is, there is little technical and functional differentiation between its product, and those of its competitors. The company has a world market share exceeding 75 percent. In order to promote the usage of its primary product, it embarks into a very extensive new product development effort *for its customers*. For instance, in the case of a nickel, chromium, or molybdenum supplier, it develops several stainless steels which contain substantial amounts of its primary product.

The business strategy that justifies this effort has a dual base. First, the development of new products for primary customers and the attendant application engineering activities expand the markets for the primary product, thus ensuring continuing growth. To be sure, the market expansion benefits the competitors as well, but this issue is not alarming as long as the company has the lion's share of the market. Secondly, the new product development effort, which is a major customer support activity, reinforces the company position in the market.

As time went by, the discovery of new mineral deposits and the development of new processing technologies helped the competition, with attendant decrease in market share for Metalcom, Inc. As such share approached the 50 percent mark, Metalcom, Inc. changed its policy. It progressively decreased new product development activities for the benefit of its customers and channeled some resources to the development of new primary products which were differentiated from those of its competitors. For instance, it developed metal powders of exacting physical characteristics and superpurity grades of its basic commodity. Alternatively it could have attempted to integrate forward, by developing and producing special types of stainless steels in competition with its customers. This strategy is, however, risky as long as the primary commodity product is essential for the financial health of the company.

This example shows that effective new product development needs not concern only the primary products manufactured and sold by a company. It also emphasizes the need to change strategies and tactics as the environment changes.

### Plasma Arc Coatings

A classic case of diversification concerns Union Carbide's Linde Division, a leading supplier of industrial gases which were primarily fungible commodities. One of Linde's diversification projects, which also helped to expand markets for industrial gases, concerned the development of plasma arc coating technologies. In an electric arc, virtually all materials melt, even ceramics. When the molten material is carried at high velocity by a gas jet, it can be deposited with reasonable uniformity and satisfactory adherence onto a substrate. Linde succeeded in developing such a process, thereby generating a separate business based on sales of coating equipment and coating services. It was an outstanding success for this pioneering organization, and also contributed enormously over the years to the advancement of materials engineering.

The success of this new product development project was partially due to management style. Linde carried out this project in a separate facility, under separate management; and treated this project, since its early years, as an *intrapreneurial venture*, rather than as a segment of its overall research and development (R&D) program.

One cannot underestimate the importance of the clear enunciation of a business strategy, of the environment in which new product development is carried out, and of management's role.

### Specialty Alloys for Aerospace

Utica Drop Forge, an independent forging shop primarily catering to low technology customers, saw new opportunities in offering its fabrication services to the aeronautical industry at the dawn of the jet age. The new potential customers were very sophisticated and demanding. As the company attempted to forge high performing alloys developed both inside and outside the aeronautical industry, it realized that the yield of saleable products was very erratic, and attributed this problem mainly to inadequate quality control of the incoming raw material.

The company's chief metallurgist, who was accountable for the solution of this technical problem, conceived a process to improve the quality control of the incoming material. But rather than coach his suppliers, he organized an internal R&D project and proved the validity of his approach. Having mastered the new process and proven product quality and industrial producibility, the company integrated backwardly and eventually expanded its new product line.

Utica Drop Forge was later acquired by the much larger Kelsey Hayes Corporation—primarily an automotive industry supplier. Kelsey Hayes recognized the business potential of the new product and process development and invested substantial funds to build the most modern plant in the world, catering exclusively to the needs of the aeronautical industry, and more specifically to those of jet engine manufacturers. This investment yielded a very handsome return.

Kelsey Hayes soon realized that the highly sophisticated operation and the customer structure of the newly created Special Metals Division did not fit in the scheme of overall corporate strategy. Therefore, it allowed the general manager (who was the former chief metallurgist) to spin off the division as an independent corporation, Special Metals, Inc., which continued a relentless new product development effort and became the world's leader in this product line. Its products found applications in a variety of advanced engineered systems, from the first supersonic jet engine, to the first rocket that brought man to the moon.

This example emphasizes the importance of early recognition of business opportunities, technical and marketing company strengths, and appropriate managerial style.

## Conclusions

"Stretch your head to the sky, but keep your feet on the ground," exhorted one of my mentors. Successful new product development rests on three pillars: planning, technology, and marketing. But successful new product development also needs superior imagination tempered by a sense of realism.

In closing, we refer again to Figure P.1 and its questions that should be answered in the order given and before substantial resources are committed.

- WHY?    Define business strategies and consider how you will evaluate successes and failures.
- WHAT?   Define the products you want to develop and the market needs they are expected to satisfy.
- HOW?    Define the implementation modes, from both the technical and the commercial viewpoints.
- WHO?    Define who is accountable for what and never lose sight of the interfunctional nature of new product development.

• WHEN? In all your new product development endeavors, be very sensitive to timing.

## Note

1. Gerd D. Wallenstein, *Concept & Practice of Product Planning* (New York: American Management Association, Inc., 1968), 15–22.

# 2

# Financial Rewards

## Introduction

A financial reward is the ultimate goal of all new product development endeavors; but to expect a direct and immediate financial reward from each new product developed is not only unreasonable, it is unwise. Most business enterprises have complex structures which, in time, develop in a somewhat erratic fashion. Whatever order is embedded in these structures becomes apparent only when it is considered over an extensive period of time.

There are many immediate and contingent reasons for developing any one product. For instance, product development may be merely a means to survival, in view of severe competitive pressures. In other cases, it implements a strategy based on a loss leader—that is, the launching of an unprofitable new product in order to entice the market to accept other lucrative products, or to enhance the company's image. A product can be continuously profitless, but only if it makes possible the marketing of supporting products. Before the days of disposable or electric razors, most shaving implements were profitless items; the profit stream was generated by the razor blades. Many medical and analytical instruments do not generate substantial profit, unless they are considered together with the consumables that are required for their operation.

Why consider financial rewards? Why learn about accounting methods? Can new product development be assessed in financial terms, so that ranking of different options, and selection of the most promising programs can be effected?

It is imperative for the *destiny planners* to understand the financial repercussions of the new product development process. They will consider primarily two issues: what is likely to happen when a business project is completed and what maximum exposure is likely to materialize during its implementation. They will consider a new product in the context of the total product portfolio and of the long-range business plans.

The comptroller assesses in more details the new product development process in terms of the cash outflow that it requires, and the financial reward that it may generate.

The product developers must at least understand the comptroller's language, in order to better relate with the financial officer and the general manager. They can do so with a minimum of effort and, if their attitude is appropriate, without disturbing primary responsibilities.

This chapter is designed to assist the product developer by presenting

- the essence of pertinent accounting principles, with emphasis on the *time value of money*,
- ways to evaluate alternative projects, and
- important issues related to new product planning and implementation.

## Elements of Accounting

The product developers should become familiar with the principal accounting reports of their companies and of their direct competitors. In the simplest case, where a company is publicly owned and has essentially a single product line, three reports are generated: the income statement, the balance sheet, and the source and disposition of funds statement.

The income statement gives revenue, operating expenses, and other expenses, wherefrom operating income and net income are derived.

What is most significant from the new product developer's viewpoint? Is the operation profitable? If not, are cost reduction projects more important or urgent than new product development projects? Is the company profitable? If not, is the red ink caused by normal operation or unusual charges? How do new product development expenses compare with total general and administrative costs? Can the income statement be segmented according to product lines?

The balance sheet gives a picture of the financial health of the establishment. Assets and liabilities are stated and subdivided into *current*, that is, those having a life shorter than one year, and the others. The relation between the funds derived from long-term borrowing and those originating from stockholder equity indicates the extent of leverage. The higher the leverage, the riskier the operation and the larger the required rate of return on the stockholder investments (assuming the operation is profitable). The balance sheet gives the new product developers a feel for the overall business risk and therefore helps them to exercise judgment about alternative projects (e.g., long-term versus short-term; cash generators versus growth-oriented).

Those unfamiliar with financial management seldom appreciate that a profitable company can run out of cash and, at times, go bankrupt. In certain circumstances, an excessive growth rate is not sustainable without exposure to enormous risks, even if profit margins are significant. The statement of sources and disposition of funds addresses the issue of liquidity. To operate properly, a business enterprise needs not only a fixed capital for plants and machinery, but also a working capital. The working capital is cash that is used like a storage tank in a water distribution system. Even if the water inflow equals or exceeds the water outflow over a period of time, the system cannot operate without a storage tank which takes care of transient increases in outflow.

From the three statements, one can derive a number of indices that define the character and risk of an enterprise. Among these are:

- Sales—this is the gross revenue. New products should contribute revenue which is significant when compared to total revenue.
- Net Profit—it consists of gross revenue minus cost of producing good, general, marketing and administrative expenses, depreciation and amortization, taxes, negative interests, and nonrecurring charges.
- Current Assets to Current Liability Ratio—this ratio, computed from balance sheet information, is one of the indices of liquidity risks. Generally, if this ratio is less than 1, the operation is very risky; however, the degree of risk depends on the type of business.
- Long-Term Debt to Total Capital Ratio—this ratio gives the extent of leverage of the establishment. A ratio higher than 0.5 indicates a substantial risk; but much depends on how predictable the future cash flow is.
- Interest Expenses to Net Cash In-Flow Ratio—being unable to cover interest expenses results in financial stresses ranging from increased cost of borrowing to drying up of cash sources. A ratio higher than 0.25 constitutes a significant risk. In recent times, we have seen ratios much higher than 0.5, e.g., in the case of leveraged buy-outs.

The income, balance sheet, and cash flow statements of an establishment give factual information; useful, but not sufficient. What accounting principles should one know that relate directly to a specific new product development project? Primarily the method called discounted cash flow analysis. This method takes into account the time value of money and, thereby, makes the developer sensitive to the importance of saving as much time as possible (consistent with the achievement of the technical and commercial goals) during the development process.

The discounted cash flow method is based on the principle that a dollar earned or spent in the future is worth less than a dollar earned or spent today. How much more or less it is worth is based on a subjective parameter which we shall call the discount rate (DR) of the project. This rate is related to the current or projected cost of borrowing money and on the risk of the project. For a totally riskless project (and there are none), a reasonable discount rate is the prevailing interest rate of United States government bonds.

The subjective discount rate can be gauged based on a rate somewhat higher than the interest that an establishment must pay to acquire adequate working capital. Whatever criterion one chooses, as of today, most new product development managers are likely to select a rate of 15 to 30 percent. Let us see now the consequences of two choices within this range. At 15 percent, the future value of one dollar of today is 50 cents six years hence, and 28 cents ten years in the future. At 30 percent, the same dollar will be worth only 27 cents six years hence, and 9 cents ten years in the future.

The future value (FV) of a present dollar is computed from the present value (PV) as follows:

$$FV = PV/(1 + DR/100)^{(N-1)}$$

where DR is the discount rate (as defined) expressed in percent, and N is the project year. Thus, for instance, in the sixth year and for a discount rate of 15 percent, $FV = PV/1.15^5$.

An example will clarify these concepts. Consider a new product development project that has an arbitrary life of ten years. In the first year, substantial technical development expenses must be sustained. These will continue at a much reduced rate in the following two years. In the third year the project begins to generate some revenue which increases in the fourth year, but drastically decreases in the fifth because of an unanticipated technical problem. This situation requires additional development costs. In the sixth year revenues resume and thereafter they begin to grow substantially, whereas development costs subside. Finally in the ninth year, the product reaches maturity and revenues level off, even though the quantities sold keep increasing. The project is discontinued after the tenth year and the investment liquidated, yielding a net cash inflow.

This rather common pattern is quantified in Table 2.1. In the second column of this table, the yearly cash inflows and outflows are stated. In the third column, labeled "Nondiscounted," the net yearly and cumulated cash flows are computed. This column does not consider the time value of money and therefore these computations are not significant.

In the other columns, net yearly and cumulative cash flows are computed, respectively, for a 20 percent and a 30 percent discount rate.

Table 2.1 gives four additional parameters:

- The *net present value* (NPV) of the project after termination and liquidation. This value (positive in the case of 20 percent discount rate and negative in the case of the 30 percent) means that after receiving a return on investment commensurate with the risk, the project has added to the establishment's wealth in the case of the 20 percent computation, whereas it has decreased the establishment's wealth in the case of the 30 percent.

- The *maximum commitment* indicates the maximum exposure that the establishment is likely to sustain if it wants to bring the project to fruition. Note that such maximum exposure is not especially sensitive to the selection of the discount rate, and therefore, of the assumed risk of the project.

- The *payback time* is the number of years after which the establishment has reached breakeven; that is, it has recovered all the cash outflow and has obtained an adequate return on investments.

## Table 2.1.
## Example of Discounted Cash Flow Analysis of a Ten-Year Project

| PROJECT YEAR | YEARLY CASH FLOW | | CASH FLOW | | | | | |
|---|---|---|---|---|---|---|---|---|
| | | | NONDISCOUNTED | | DISC. AT 20% | | DISC. AT 30% | |
| | IN | OUT | YEARLY | CUMUL. | YEARLY | CUMUL. | YEARLY | CUMUL. |
| 1 | 0 | 500 | −500 | −500 | −500.0 | −500.0 | −500.0 | −500.0 |
| 2 | 0 | 50 | −50 | −550 | −41.7 | −541.7 | −38.5 | −538.5 |
| 3 | 100 | 20 | 80 | −470 | 55.6 | −486.1 | 47.3 | −491.1 |
| 4 | 200 | 0 | 200 | −270 | 115.7 | −370.4 | 91.0 | −400.1 |
| 5 | 50 | 100 | −50 | −320 | −24.1 | −394.5 | −17.5 | −417.6 |
| 6 | 200 | 10 | 190 | −130 | 76.4 | −318.1 | 51.2 | −366.4 |
| 7 | 300 | 0 | 300 | 170 | 100.5 | −217.6 | 62.2 | −304.3 |
| 8 | 450 | 0 | 450 | 620 | 125.6 | −92.0 | 71.7 | −232.6 |
| 9 | 500 | 0 | 500 | 1120 | 116.3 | 24.3 | 61.3 | −171.3 |
| 10 | 500 | 0 | 500 | 1620 | 96.9 | 121.2 | 47.1 | −124.1 |
| 10 LIQ. | 100 | 20 | 80 | 1700 | 15.5 | 136.7 | 7.5 | −116.6 |

| NPV AFTER LIQUIDATION | 1700 | 136.7 | −116.6 |
|---|---|---|---|
| MAXIMUM COMMITTMENT | 550 | 541.7 | 538.5 |
| PAYBACK TIME (YEARS) | 6.3 | 8.5 | >10 |

INTERNAL RATE OF RETURN
24.6%

- The *internal rate of return* (IRR) is the discount rate that, if it were selected, would make the payback time equal to the life of the project, and therefore would make the net present value at the end of the project equal to zero. The internal rate of return is a parameter that permits a comparison among alternative projects having different lives, sizes, and other features. Caution should be exercised before using only this parameter for comparisons, as will be explained later.

The data of Table 2.1 are plotted in Figure 2.1. Note principally the dramatic effect of the discount rate on payback time and net present value.

## Where to Find Financial Information

Where can one find financial information about competitors, in these times of foreign acquisitions, mergers, and leveraged buy-outs? Not an easy task, but, in most cases, not impossible. If data bases are available, they should be un-

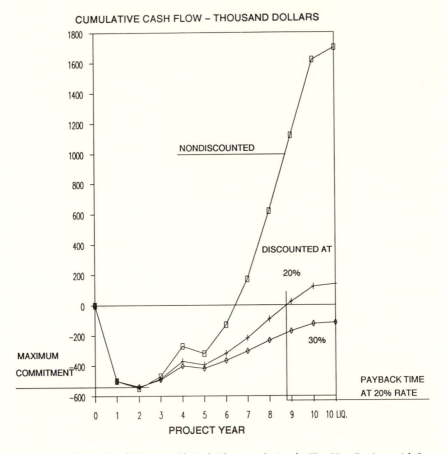

Figure 2.1 Example of Discounted Cash Flow Analysis of a Ten-Year Project with Indication of Maximum Commitment and Payback Time

covered; if they are not, they should be constructed from other information sources to the extent possible.

The Securities and Exchange Commission requires public corporations to publish at least minimal financial data. For those that are diversified, some data must be segmented according to product lines or principal types of business. Most corporations publish an annual and four quarterly reports which contain the essence of the compulsory financial data base. More is contained in "Form 10-K," an expanded version of the annual report, designed to advise the stockholders about the major risks affecting the corporation. Competitive position, product liability, pending legal actions, and other elements of the company's risks are described. Financial data are usually more detailed than those presented in the annual and quarterly reports, and, at any rate, they are displayed in a standard, numerical fashion which better permit comparison between data from two or more companies. All corporations supply copies of

Form 10-K, offered free of charge or at a nominal cost. The developer who wants to obtain a substantial number of Form 10-K, can take a shortcut by availing of services that provide copies, often by express mail, for a fee.

More details are generally contained in the prospectus that the Securities and Exchange Commission makes mandatory for companies that issue shares or bonds. A prospectus can be obtained from the appropriate underwriters and, usually, from most security brokers.

What if the companies of interest are not public? Certain private corporations voluntarily publish at least partial financial information to give their customers a sense of their character, size, stability, and potential. Failing to uncover such sources, one must resort to proprietary books and computer files or to consulting firms. Among the most valuable proprietary publications that supply at least minimal information are:

• *Ward's Business Directory*™ contains financial information on many private corporations as well as subsidiaries and divisions of large corporations.[1] It also reports on some international firms.
• *Million Dollar Directory*® lists most companies selling at least one million dollars.[2]
• *Standard and Poor's Register* lists corporations of various sizes, including some small ones not found in other directories.[3]

Much of this information can today be obtained on-line through one of the computerized information retrieval services.

Detailed financial information concerning the companies that undertake new product development is, of course, available internally, but jealously sheltered except for what must be revealed by law. Many new product developers, including middle-level managers, do not have access to this information except on a "need to know" basis.

## Discounted Cash Flow Analysis of a New Product Development Project

The development of a discounted cash flow analysis before substantial resources are committed to a new product development project is highly desirable, but how can one quantitatively assess the financial repercussions of a product that is yet to be developed? This type of problem confronts the developer very often and should not be dismissed because of the difficulties it entails. Ultimately, this problem is solved by periodic reiterations, that is, by setting a framework based on logical factors, quantifying this framework in a tentative fashion, and then refining it as the project proceeds.

The principal factors that the developer should consider include:

• Time, such as minimum time needed for technical development, time needed to design, build, and start up manufacturing facilities, anticipated rate of commercial penetration, and anticipated rate of obsolescence.

- Capital investment, which mainly depends on the adequacy of existing manufacturing and distribution facilities for the production and marketing of the new product.
- Resources needed for technical and commercial development.
- Product price assumptions, consistent with anticipated competitive reactions.
- Sales volume goals that are significant when compared with the company's total business.
- An overall risk factor, from which an appropriate discount rate is chosen.

## Evaluations

A single new product can seldom be evaluated in isolation, if for no other reason, because it is likely to affect, whether negatively or positively, other products. A business is a complex system, and any change within this system can affect the overall operation. A new product may accelerate the obsolescence of others, or can improve their market appeal because of synergistic effects. Then, should one be concerned with discounted cash flow analysis, or other methods to assess the financial repercussion of a new product?

To the extent that a new product can stand alone (ideally, to the extent that a new product constitutes a new strategic business unit), financial analysis is feasible and meaningful. We shall begin by considering this case, which, typically, concerns a company that intends to diversify outside its traditional business area by way of developing a new product.

Such company, in its earliest planning stage, is likely to consider more than one potential project, but has resources to implement, initially, only one. Before committing substantial resources, it has to choose, and, for this choice, it needs to undertake comparative analyses of its options.

Assume that there are three options and that a tentative discounted cash flow analysis is carried out for all. The only comparable parameter generated by such analysis is the internal rate of return, because the others (net present value, maximum commitment, and the payback time) are a function of the assumed discount rates which is different if the business risks of the three options are not the same.

Should one always select the option that yields the highest internal rate of return? Not necessarily. After discarding the options that yield an inadequate internal rate of return, the remaining options should be assessed based on a number of other factors as well. For a 100-million dollar company, a product expected to yield 25 percent and to generate, at maturity, sales of 20 million dollars may be preferable to one that is expected to yield 40 percent, but is unlikely to generate more than three million dollar sales. In cases where the business environment is affected by severe uncertainties, or competition is likely to respond aggressively to the introduction of a new product, one may favor the option that has a much shorter payback, even if the internal rate of return is somewhat smaller than those of other options.

Ranking may be based on a "figure of merit" which is derived from both financial and non-financial factors. To determine this figure of merit, all non-financial factors are quantified based on an arbitrary scale (e.g., from $+5$ for the most favorable, to $-5$ for the least favorable factor). Thereby, both financial and non-financial factors can be expressed in a numerical form and an overall figure of merit derived.

The ranking exercise, even in the simplest cases, should be regarded only as one element of decision making. Excessive reliance on mechanical means to select the most desirable product often leads the developer astray. There is no substitute for personal judgment, especially if derived from collective inputs.

Ranking becomes more complex if a new product cannot stand alone as a business unit. The approach to these more complex, and, for a larger establishment, more common situations is essentially the same as that of the simpler cases described above. Rather than assessing single products, a product line, or a multi-line business project should be the subject of ranking and selection. A typical situation is represented by a company that has three established product lines and is planning to improve them by adding products that have higher values added and profit margins. In this case, ranking and selection should depend on the comparison of the benefits that each line derives from the new product development effort, and not only by the financial worthiness of each new product.

In these days of mergers and acquisitions, new product development establishments are being scrutinized in terms of their effectiveness. Can two organizations be merged? Can product development be more effectively farmed out? Can the acquisition of proprietary rights held by others be a more expedient way of achieving business goals than internal development? To a certain extent, the evaluation, ranking, and selection methodologies that have been described for new products can be useful to evaluate, rank, and select organizations, or alternative ways of achieving business objectives. However, an establishment can be evaluated only over a reasonably long period of time and with regard to all the projects that it is capable of handling. This issue will be discussed more fully in the chapters concerning the implementation of technical development and its organization.

To delay evaluations and selections of alternative endeavors can lead to a waste of precious resources and time. On the other hand, a very inflexible evaluation and selection methodology may lead to a much more serious problem: the premature demise of potentially rewarding endeavors.

## Important Financial Issues

The assessment of the financial health of a company and its competitors, and the ranking of alternative new product development projects are but two endeavors that relate to the ultimate financial reward. Other important issues may be considered in order to maximize the value of the new product development process. Among these are:

- The determination of an appropriate overall level of effort, commensurate with the difficulty of the tasks at hand and with the effort exercised by the competitors.
- The partition between the technical and the commercial development levels of effort.
- The consideration of the sunken costs of a project or group of projects.

In management science literature, research and development expenses of individual companies and of industries are often expressed as a percent of sales, in order to normalize them across a number of diversified establishments. As an example, 1 percent of sales devoted to research and development is average for the metallurgical industry whereas the pharmaceutical industry spends ten times as much. The aerospace industry operates somewhat in between these two industries. Are these statistics significant? Perhaps they are, as a partial and approximate indication of what may be needed to stay in business and compete effectively, but not as a definitive gauge to be used by any member of a given industry in order to rate the adequacy of its own effort.

First, R&D expenses are not uniformly defined. In many cases, they include technical endeavors supporting manufacturing and sales of current products rather than new product development. Secondly, the percentage of such expenses that derives from corporate funds (as opposed to government or other sponsors) vary widely from industry to industry, and also within each industry. Finally, and most importantly, technical development effort is but a part of the total new product development process. The fraction of general and administrative expenses that is devoted to commercial development is difficult to determine; yet it is an essential part of the new product development process.

Initially, product planning should start without a preconceived idea of the level of effort that is required. The main concern is not to keep up with the average of the industry, or to emulate competitors with regard to application of resources. As the preliminary plan develops, approximate resources needed to keep the product portfolio in a good shape must be estimated. If these resources were not available, consideration should be given to join ventures, government's support, or other means to stretch corporate resources.

Having established the approximate resources needed to reach the ultimate goal, the next planning decision is to tentatively partition such resources between technical and commercial development endeavors. These two endeavors should occur in parallel, be intertwined or at least mutually supporting, and lead to success in an orderly fashion. One should note that resources suitable for technical and for commercial development activities are not necessarily interchangeable; but, in this regard, there is much more inherent flexibility than usually anticipated. Lack of interchangeability is often caused by removable organizational constraints rather than by the inherent capabilities of development staff and facilities.

For a variety of reasons, most companies, especially in the "high technology" industries, tend to bias the level of effort in favor of the technical development. Most new products must be promoted. Moreover, irrespective of the extent of market research, the real needs of the customers is not fully understood until the new product is on the market.

The most effective planning is based on subdividing the affordable effort into three portions; one assigned to technical development, a second to commercial development, and a third temporarily unassigned and to be biased toward the first or the second direction according to contingent needs perceived in the later stages of the new product development process.

Are sunken costs significant? The temptation to plan the future based on the expenditures of the past is great. This temptation is like a gambler who wants to try his luck once more *because* he has squandered most of his resources. The probability of hitting the jackpot in any single trial is exactly the same, whether the gambler previously lost or won. Similarly, in the case of the new product development process, what counts is the probability to hit the mark in a reasonable time frame based on *future* expenditures. The knowledge accumulated is often of value; but, such value may, at times, be higher if the original project is abandoned (irrespective of its sunken costs) and the knowledge is applied to a more promising project.

## Examples

The following examples are designed to clarify the principal concepts and issues described above. The first (*Labelking*) emphasizes the interpretation of the financial statements of two competitive companies, one of which is planning to develop a new product. The second (*Speedy*) and the third (*Mining*) highlight the value of the discounted cash flow analysis at the early stages of new product planning.

### Labelking

Labelking (a fictitious corporation) has been a supplier of labels, mainly for industrial and commercial applications, but also for consumers, since the turn of the century. Its conservative management led the corporation to growth and profitability, mainly by following, with caution, the pace setting actions of its competitors. It has, however, recognized business opportunities and has developed several new product lines, some of which are technologically sophisticated. For instance, it recognized the potential of optical scanning. The company launched an optical scanning label product line and later decided to diversify into the optical scanning equipment by negotiating a joint venture with a leading corporation.

Labelking's director of planning, searching for new business opportunities compatible with the company's technical and marketing strengths, observed that high technology has succeeded in expediting and improving label reading for items ranging from library books to supermarket grocery, movement of railroad cars, and baggage handling, but did not affect a very important area—airline tickets. The director of planning observed that some progress was made because airline tickets are now printed by a computer which is connected with reservation, accounting, and other data bases, but further improvement is possible.

The director of planning consulted with the technical director, asking whether a new product that overcomes the drawbacks of the present system could be developed. After meeting with his specialists, the technical director responded that the system could indeed be improved, but current technology (e.g., optical scanning) was unlikely to be adequate. A brainstorming session concluded that the only hope (by no means assurance) was to depend on holography. Holography was practiced commercially, for instance to add security to credit cards, and fundamentally depended on laser technology with which Labelking was comfortable. The technical director could not even begin to estimate the resources needed and the probability of success, but stated that the development was certainly expensive, very time consuming, and technically risky.

As a preliminary step in assessing whether to recommend a project on airline tickets, the director of planning compared the financial statement of his company with that of the most aggressive and competent competitor, Topflight. The results of that cursory competitive analysis are given in Table 2.2.

Obviously, Topflight was a powerful competitor that had devoted substantial resources to technical developments. It was, however, more leveraged, as indicated by the long-term debt to total capital ratio. Further analysis of financial statements and other reports indicated that Topflight had a sustained growth rate because that competitor succeeded in translating the positive results of its substantial technical effort into commercial successes.

Was this information sufficient to make a go/no-go decision on the airline ticket project? Certainly not. But it was adequate to indicate that a competitive reaction to the launching of an airline ticket project was most likely to occur, and that the somewhat riskier financial position of Topflight was unlikely to deter this competitor from pursuing the same path.

### Speedy

Speedy, a fictitious small company selling a specialized software product line, conceived a new product that increased the speed of computation of a popular personal computer hardware by a factor ten.

From past experience, it estimated the resources and the time needed to commercialize the invention after the end of the technical development. Technical development needed the acquisition of some capital items, whose costs were reasonably predictable.

Table 2.2.
Preliminary Competitive Analysis of Key Financial Indicators

| FACTOR | LABELKING | TOPFLIGHT |
|---|---|---|
| NET SALES (MILLION $/YR.) | 700 | 1400 |
| NET EARNINGS (MILLION $/YR.) | 34 | 75 |
| NET EARNINGS (PERCENT OF NET SALES) | 4.85 | 5.15 |
| R&D EXPENDITURES (MILLION $/YR.) | 15 | 50 |
| LONG TERM DEBT/TOTAL CAPITAL | 0.31 | 0.45 |
| CURR. ASSETS/CURR. LIABILITIES | 2.15 | 1.75 |
| INTERESTS/NET CASH FLOW | 0.18 | 0.35 |

Speedy's general manager estimated the time needed to carry out the technical development, set a goal for the minimum sales volume that would make the project significant, in the context of his company's total business, monitored competitive activities, and concluded that his preliminary business plan was sound.

The general manager decided, at this point, to undertake a discounted cash flow analysis of this project, and, from a perception of the business risk, selected a discount rate of 25 percent and chose a project life of only five years.

The discounted cash flow analysis clearly indicated that the net present value of this new product development project would mainly depend on the time needed to complete the technical development and bring the product to first commercialization. The general manager was convinced that the marketing would not be a principal bottleneck, once the field testing had been successfully accomplished. Based on this cursory analysis, the general manager asked his technical director to explore how the time needed for technical development could be decreased, either by increasing the internal resources, or by acquiring proprietary right of software that could expedite the technical development.

## Mining

This example describes a generic case. A typical mining operation is very capital intensive, that is, the ratio of total capital to yearly revenue is very large. As much as five dollars of capital may be needed to obtain one dollar per year revenue. In addition, the revenue stream does not begin to flow for several years after the launching of the project.

A discounted cash flow analysis in the planning stage is imperative in this case. To optimize the cash flow, only a part of the total capital needed is invested in the beginning of the project and a partial revenue is obtained as soon as practicable. For instance, the planner may select to sell initially a natural product, such as ore concentrate, and to delay the investment for a smelting and refining plant. This plan temporarily sacrifices part of the value added, but accelerates the beginning of cash inflow.

Discounted cash flow can also be useful to test another common feature of capital intensive operations. A new plant of this kind does not operate properly when first started because of its complexity; therefore, the planner includes in its cash flow analysis resources for plant start-up. By increasing the technical development costs, the start-up costs tend to decrease; thus, several choices can be made in this regard, each based on levels of expenditures and timing. The discounted cash flow analysis is helpful to undertake a preliminary optimization with regard to the balance between technical development and start-up costs.

## Conclusions

A facet of the "WHY?" question in new product development concerns the financial reward at the end of the line. Financial reward derives from commercial success, cost control, and defense against competitive activities. As a new product development project evolves, and especially in its later phases, the factors determining the ultimate financial success become more clear, and appropriate actions can be planned, standing on sound bases. Not so in the initial phases of a project, and, even less when the goal is to select between alternative products or projects or approaches *before* committing substantial resources.

In the early stage of the product development process three exercises are recommended. The first concerns the financial environment of the company developing a new product and its competitors (current and potential) in the same product line. The financial environment is assessed by perusing published and other financial information, and deriving from that an estimation of financial strength, financial risk, ability to capitalize on successes, financial repercussions of failures, research and development capabilities, and many other factors, as they relate to the specific product or products being considered.

The second exercise consists of estimating, in a preliminary fashion, the cash inflow and outflow, and its timing, caused by the technical and commercial development activities. Precise assessment is impossible at these early times; however, three alternative scenarios (pessimistic, most likely, and optimistic) may be constructed. The cash flow analysis should include the transition period from first commercialization to firm establishment, and consider as well the maturing and declining stages of the new product. A business project based on the new product must have a finite life. The analysis should consider the time value of money, and therefore be carried out on a *discounted* basis. This exercise indicates the maximum exposure, the net present value, the payback time, and other parameters that can be used first to determine whether the project is worth pursuing (or which project should be selected among various alternatives), and then to improve the development plan by affecting those parameters that have the strongest effect on the ultimate financial reward.

The third exercise concerns the partition of the total new product development effort between technical and commercial. Because of the overlapping of technical and commercial activities, such partition is initially tentative and approximate. Financial reward is often improved by biasing the effort toward commercial development activities, whereas, naturally, the intriguing enticement of technology development tends to favor that facet of the total effort. Here the judicious use of impartial assessors (e.g., company directors or consultants) may be highly desirable.

Whatever numbers can be generated in these three exercises will help to sharpen the perception of the task at hand. However, qualitative assessments and intuitive feelings should not be dismissed, and, first of all, mechanical analyses of much complexity should be avoided.

## Notes

The author is indebted to Dr. Firoze Katrak of Charles River Associates, Incorporated for his helpful comments on this chapter.

1. *Ward's Business Directory*™ *of Major International Companies* (Belmont, California: Information Access Company, Division of Ziff Davis Publishing Co., 1988).

2. *Million Dollar Directory.*® *America's Leading Public and Private Companies* (Parsippany, New Jersey: The Dun & Bradstreet Corporation, 1989).

3. *Standard & Poor's Register of Corporations, Directors, and Executives* (New York, New York: Standard & Poor's Corporation, a McGraw-Hill Financial Service Company, 1989).

## PART II

# WHAT?—PRODUCT DEFINITION

# 3

---

# Market Pull

## Introduction

We have established the principal motivations for new product development, the "WHY." Defining the principal target, the "WHAT," is the next logical step in the new product development process.

All business enterprises must sell something to somebody. Therefore, it behooves the new product developer to identify one or more products or services that the market needs. These wants constitute the market pull. Management science literature has been arguing whether innovations principally derive from market pull or technology push. Are these two drivers collaborative, antagonistic, or independent of each other?

Most arguments concerning the superiority of either driver are sterile, because, at least in the industrially developed countries, technology is always pushing and concomitantly market needs always cry for their fulfillment. Thus, both drivers are active all the time, albeit to different extents according to contingent situations.

Fundamentally, the market pull relates to the product function, whereas the technology push concerns the way of executing such function. Take, as an example, the need to communicate reliably and with adequate privacy. This need has existed since the dawn of civilization, but has changed in character as mankind developed in a variety of ways. This development changed the specific characteristics of communication needs, with regard to distance, speed, and content. Technology catered to these changes by designing new or improved ways of fulfilling the basic communication function. Technology also created new needs while satisfying others.

Facsimile transmission, for instance (commonly called "telefaxing"), offers high reliability, speed, flexibility, and modest cost. Because of these features, many important business transactions are now delayed until the very last minute, and this makes the use of telefaxing imperative. What was reserved for exceptional circumstances has become a fairly routine manner of communicating.

How can we define market pull in environments which are so complex and changeable? The new product developer must define, at first, the market pull in a qualitative manner. Why qualitative? Can one plan soundly without establishing quantitative dimensions?

These questions are answered by a simile. The French philosopher Henri Bergson in his *Philosophy of Intuition* emphasized that one thousand picture cards of Paris cannot give the feel for that great city that a look at Paris gives. To the uninitiated, discrete details may be disturbing or at least ineffective until an intuitive appreciation is gained. Thus, the travelers who have never been to Paris and intend to plan a visit to that city should first look at an aerial photograph or at a comprehensive map. It serves no useful purpose to first determine how far the Tuileries is from their hotel.

Likewise, the new product developer should first develop a feel for the task at hand. A good way to start is to understand qualitative market needs. Quantitative market parameters are eventually essential, but they should be determined later.

The preliminary and qualitative assessment of market needs must be founded on the conviction that market needs are not absolute and unchangeable; they are always subjective and dynamic.

Assume that a manufacturer wants to develop a better process control system. A product manager calls on a potential customer and talks to people at the customer's site, in the operation, engineering, and purchasing departments. The night shift plant superintendent emphasizes the needs for manufacturing controls that are reliable and forgiving. After all, night shift workers may not be as alert as day shift workers and supporting infrastructures are very lean at night. Errors can be very costly. The day shift superintendent is less conservative and wants to achieve maximum productivity by driving the operating system to its ultimate capabilities, even if production is occasionally interrupted. A design engineering manager wants to know about the most flexible and sophisticated control system that your company has developed. The purchasing director has little sympathy for the concern of the other managers. He wants to buy what is adequate, not what is best. These conflicting needs must be taken into account by the manufacturer who wants to develop a better process control system.

The subjective nature of definition of needs is not restricted to the customer's environment and organizational structure. Conflicts may derive from differences between private and public interests. Countless examples could be quoted regarding products that would have strong market appeal in the private sector, if it were not for issues concerning safety, security, environmental impacts, or international politics. The repercussions of these issues will be expounded in the next chapter because the limitations imposed by the public sector are not necessarily negative; they often constitute major sources of new product ideas.

The different viewpoints of manufacturers, distributors, retailers, and service organizations also generate contrasting definitions of market needs. Therefore, it is not sufficient to identify what the ultimate customers want. The developer must understand the structure of the distribution channels even before defining the new products, thereby assuring that such product can effectively be brought to market.

Market needs are not only subjective. They are also dynamic. They continually change and are affected by changes in the environment. Is a new product likely to be affected by the cost of energy, government regulations, currency exchange rate, mergers, or life-styles? Does the market appeal of utilitarian houses change if the land value suddenly increases? Will customers be able to dispose of new products without incurring substantial expenses?

The Greek philosopher Heraclitus admonished that one cannot dip his hand in a river twice, because the second time the river has changed. Similarly, the product developer cannot cater to a market need twice. The market and its needs have changed in the interim, at times because of the introduction of the new product.

## Product Definition

A developer must define new products prior to expenditure of substantial development resources. Precise and quantitative definitions can seldom be stated in the earliest stages of the new product development process. At best, such definitions are likely to be tentative and semi-quantitative. They can and should be refined as the process continues.

New product definition must focus on function rather than on physical or other characteristics. When customers buy computers and its operating software, they are principally concerned about performance. How fast? What memory capacity? How reliable? How user friendly? They may even ask the question: would a programmable hand calculator serve our needs? In our complex, technology-driven society, a market need is often satisfied not only by a variety of products, but also by several, entirely different systems and structures. Microwave long distance communication can fulfill essentially the same need as fiber optics. Telemarketing may substitute for travel. Robots can take the place of labor. Capital may be traded for energy consumption.

Functionality is especially important when one attempts to differentiate a new product from prior art. In an underdeveloped country a computer is unlikely to fulfill a grocer's needs better than an abacus or a simple calculator. A software product capable of operating in six different environments may be functionally less appealing than six separate softwares, each capable of operating in a single environment.

After gaining a feel for the functions required by the market need, the potential new product should be defined in terms of its specific elements. A simplified picture of the principal elements of product definition is given in Figure 3.1. The following paragraphs describe each element.

The issue of industrial producibility is often neglected in the early stage of the new product development process because engineering design has not pro-

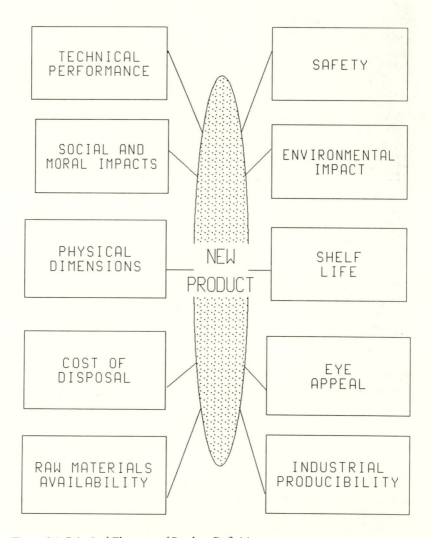

Figure 3.1 Principal Elements of Product Definition

gressed beyond the conceptual stage. It is imperative to analyze this issue as soon as practicable. Any product depends on a manufacturing process. Even "soft products" such as computer software must eventually be mass produced. Even services (e.g., electronic banking) depend on processes.

Any new process, in turn, depends on many technologies that are well established and on a few that must be developed if the new product is not to be relegated to the role of a laboratory curiosity. The product developer must identify these enabling technologies or success factors before committing substantial resources.

Consider, as an example, the development of integrated circuits based on gallium arsenide. The first item to be analyzed is the availability of raw material at a reasonable price. A quick survey will indicate that supplies are adequate, at least in the short term. Then one should consider scale-up problems, that is, technical and nontechnical issues that are likely to arise as the new product graduates from development to commercial status. The feasibility of producing large crystals of adequate perfection is, in this case, a principal concern. Other issues relate to the disposal of waste streams created by the process, the disposal of post-consumer products, occupational safety and health, and environmental impact.

Physical dimensions and eye appeal are more or less critical according to each specific product and market niche. Physical dimensions has become a progressively more important issue in recent times. Once bigness was extolled; now, perhaps because of the pervasive impact of microelectronics, smallness is usually preferred. The reduction of physical dimensions is consistent with today's style of life and also leads to a significant decrease in transportation and storage costs. Eye appeal is most important for consumers' products; but is also critical for institutional and industrial products. Medical instruments, for example, must have an image projecting cleanliness and reliability. Surfaces must be easily cleanable even when affected by reagents; long-term storage in tropical warehouses must not lead to staining due to mildew.

The last and most difficult element to consider is the social and moral impact of new products. Here difficulties arise from several sources. Society is diversified; yet certain elements of society have an out-of-proportion influence on the molding of what is acceptable and proper. These elements emerge, and at times become submerged; their impact is often unpredictable or surprising.

Nuclear power generation is a case in point. At first, nuclear power reactors were hailed as a way of generating unlimited quantities of electricity independently of foreign fuel supplies. The nuclear and the uranium mining industries grew and appeared to be heading for ever-expanding opportunities. Then the Three Mile Island accident occurred and reminded us of the risks that nuclear power entailed. Negative social reaction was very strong, and led to constraints that prompted the cancellation of several ongoing projects and the cost escalation of the surviving projects. Then came Chernobyl, and the nuclear power industry appeared to be headed for eventual obliteration. But not so. As the so-called greenhouse effect—the warming trend of the earth with dire consequences on agriculture, flooding, and other vital environmental issues—was publicized, society realized that the choice is often between two evils. Nuclear power no longer looked so ominous in the light of the newly acquired knowledge about its alternatives. Whereas opposition still prevailed, certain projects that were in jeopardy were reinstated. We dare predict that nuclear power has survived societal scrutiny and is on its way to recovery, at least in the short term; but no assurances can be made for the long term. This is another demonstration of the dynamic nature of market needs.

Figure 3.1 is only a tentative framework. New product developers should use this list of product definition elements as a point of departure, adding others that are critical and specific to the task at hand, and possibly deleting those that are not significant in their specific contexts.

The early product definition must be continuously refined in the course of the new product development process in a reiterative fashion, as additional information becomes available from technical and market research. Progressively, the new product profile will become sharper and its various elements will become definable in quantitative terms. The reiterative nature of this exercise is also typical of many other endeavors that the product developer should carry out in the course of his activities.

## Sources of Market Needs

The sources of market needs are specific, but certain generalizations are feasible, because they help to become oriented while searching for opportunities among a large number of diversified options. Initially, product planning should depend on a broad perspective and be independent of preconceived ideas or on premature definition of specific market targets. These generalizations are indeed difficult and occasionally may lead astray; yet, on balance, they should be attempted.

The first generalization concerns industrial products, that is, those products that do not reach the consumer directly, but are instrumental in fulfilling the needs of their underlying markets. In these cases (see Figure 3.2), the principal sources of market needs are, generally:

- Fulfillment of unique functions,
- Improved effectiveness of customers' products,
- Improved efficiency of customers' operations, and
- Need to respond to government regulations and other external events affecting customers' operations.

As operations and products become increasingly more complex and technologically sophisticated, the fulfillment of unique functions becomes preeminent among the sources of market needs. These needs are the easiest to identify and those on which most attention is paid by new product developers. Microelectronics offers countless examples. For instance, in the microwave area, the industry has moved toward higher and higher operational frequencies. One way of achieving this goal has been the development of a device (the so-called IMPATT diode) that, however, generates intense heat in a very small

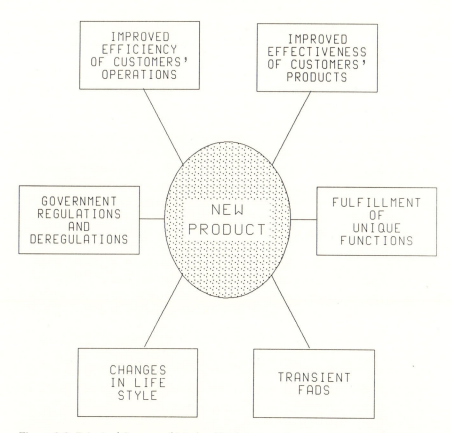

Figure 3.2 Principal Sources of Market Needs

area of the device—so intense, in fact, that it could cause alterations impairing the operation. In this case, the market needs can be satisfied in one of two ways. One is, obviously, to design a different device of similar performance, but free from hot spots or more heat resistant. These developments have been attempted with reasonable success, but, so far, have not achieved the level of operational frequencies desired. The other approach is to use a material having the unique function of extracting heat very promptly and effectively, while not interfering with the functioning of the device. Such materials must have several technical features; one feature is electrical insulation. The best material known that combines high electrical resistivity with high thermal conductivity is diamond. From these features and limitation, the new potential product is defined as follows: a diamond wafer of given dimensions that can be embedded into, or attached to, a conductive metal such as copper. Most likely, an approximate maximum price should also be defined.

The above example is an actual case. Both natural and synthetic diamond "heat sinks" are on the market today. One can dream of other new products that could satisfy a unique function. Most, as in the case of diamond heat sinks, are to be found among those that have two seemingly contradictory features, such as strong and light, small and very complex, fast and accurate, powerful and safe.

The identification of needs concerning those products that improve the effectiveness of the customers' products implies an understanding of the customers' technical and commercial operation. All too often, suppliers are adequately aware of customers' technical operations but neglect to become knowledgeable in the downstream utilization of customers' products. How are they distributed? What functions do they perform? What services do they require? Are they ultimate products or, in turn, are they used to make other products? A review of the product integration flow sheet described in Chapter 1 is desirable as a way to become oriented. It is not sufficient, because such flow sheet concerns only products and processes. It does not include commercial development and other facets of marketing operations.

The components of an engineered system—an automobile, a power plant, a washing machine—are examples of products that may enhance the marketability of the customers' products. Their definition depends not only on their functions in the engineered system, but also on the needs of distributors, service organizations, customers' customers. For instance, the supplier of integrated circuits used in a telephone exchange needs to understand their performance in terms of the service that the telephone company offers to its subscribers.

Improved effectiveness of customers' operations is a major source of market needs and would be the easiest to analyze (because benefits are direct) if it were not for the proprietary secrecy that shrouds most industrial processes. One can, however, scout for market needs by considering that most industrially feasible operations depend on raw materials, energy, labor, and fixed capital. Each element generates a cost. The understanding of the relative significance of these costs helps to become sensitive to what is most important to the customer. Another feature that is usually very important to industrial operators is flexibility. Can the level of operation be decreased or increased within relatively broad limits without affecting average unit costs? Can the same operation be suitable for the manufacture of several products without a time-consuming or expensive changeover? Is the equipment difficult to operate when skilled labor is in short supply? Can the equipment be upgraded without major investments?

Improved effectiveness of customers' operation also depends on government regulations. These factors will be considered in more detail in the next chapter because they constitute one of the principal sources of new product ideas. Collectively, they may be called mandated markets.

The approach described above for industrial products often applies also to consumer products, especially with regard to needs deriving from improvement in customers' operations, and from sensitivity to government regulations. Consumer products are, however, affected by additional factors, of which change of life-style is dominant.

We are living in a rapidly changeable society. We witness these changes both in our domestic environment and abroad. A case in point is the westernization of the Pacific region, with attending new needs. (See, for instance, the very rapid growth of soft drink consumption in Japan.) Domestically we have witnessed changes in life-style ranging from attire (see the transformation of the old-fashioned sneaker to computer-designed, high performance sporting shoes, specifically aimed at a single function) to eating habits, such as the change from one square meal in the evening to the habit of "grazing" whenever time allows.

In his lucid paper, Sharrard[1] outlined "the long-term multifold trend of Western Civilization." Among the trends quoted there, the following are especially pertinent to the definition of market needs. Cultures are becoming sensate, that is, more pragmatic, rational, utilitarian, and secular. Technological changes are institutionalized. Military capabilities increase and spread to a number of underdeveloped nations. In the industrialized countries, affluence and leisure are on an upswing. Urbanization is increasing, leading to the creation of megalopolises. The importance of primary occupations is decreasing, while the importance of secondary, tertiary, and other occupations is increasing. Literacy and education are increasing; the consumer is becoming more knowledgeable and demands explanations on the consequences of using a new product. Finally, the tempo of these and other changes is accelerating.

The awareness of these and other societal trends helps to define market needs and to consider what is likely to happen to the environment during the life of the new products.

Should the definition of military market needs follow a different methodology? Only partially. The previously enunciated guidelines are valid. However, two additional unique features characterize military market needs. Such needs are often unattainable based on present state of the art, and they can be defined only partially because of national security considerations.

The perusal of several Strategic Defense Initiative Organization's requests for proposal can vouch for the unattainability of certain military needs; yet significant business opportunities may originate from such developments (even if the original goal is never attained), either because the development programs constitute, per se, a sizable business, or because by-products can be commercialized.

The secrecy issue is a potential problem mainly because of the complications and expenses involved to obtain clearances. Therefore, involvement in classified projects has to be substantial. A potential supplier cannot stay on the sidelines and effectively offer limited products. More generally, the definition of military market needs is most effective if the supplier of potential new products is constantly and intimately involved, by way of furnishing other products, or in other manners, with the organizations that are likely to become customers.

# Examples

Two examples are given to reinforce the concepts enunciated in the preceding sections of this chapter. *Catalytic Converter* identifies the many sources of market needs caused by a single legislation that limited the emission from automotive vehicles. *Telecommunication Networks* emphasizes the necessity of focusing on the functional definition of a new product.

### Catalytic Converter

Two U.S. government organizations, the Environmental Protection Agency (EPA) and the Occupational Health and Safety Administration (OSHA), have generated countless new market needs in recent years.

The automotive industry has been a prime target of the environmental controllers, and for a very good reason. The gasoline engine emits noxious gases, including carbon monoxide, nitrogen oxides, and unburned hydrocarbons. It also emits tolerable amounts of particulate matter. The diesel engine, on the other hand, emits large amounts of particulate matter, but tolerable amounts of noxious gases. With over 180 million vehicles registered in the United States alone, and with the high concentration in urban areas, something had to be done to decrease this emission because of its deleterious effects on people. More recently, this concern was extended to secondary effects, such as the so-called acid rain and its impact on wildlife and vegetation, even though auto emission is not, in this regard, the major culprit.

EPA attacked the major problem first, and imposed emission standards for gasoline engines only. The earlier standards could be met by engine modifications; but, as the standards became tighter, the cleaning of the exhaust gases became necessary.

Gas cleaning has been practiced by the chemical and metallurgical industries for a long time, but the domestic automotive industry could not transfer this technology directly because of major constraints, including space limitation, weight limitations (added weight decreases mileage) and cost. The task at hand was aggravated by the fact that certain foreign auto manufacturers were able to produce cars that met EPA standards without modifications.

This problem was solved by adding a component, the catalytic converter, whose function is to destroy some of the obnoxious constituents of the exhaust gases, transforming them into acceptable emissions. The earlier converters cleaned carbon monoxide and unburned hydrocarbon, but not nitrogen oxides. When the EPA standards were extended to cover nitrogen oxides, modifications had to be introduced to maintain the viability of the catalytic converter.

The production of catalytic converters generated additional new market needs: chromium for the stainless steel container, ceramics for the catalyst substrate, platinum group metals for the catalyst. Moreover, the converter necessitated modifications of other engine components and controls. Because lead poisons the catalyst, leaded gasoline had to be banned, and the petroleum industry had to develop a new product: unleaded gasoline of high octane number. The third pump appeared and with it a higher priced gasoline. In turn, the new gasoline required new kinds of catalysts for its refining process.

We have seen, in the above, how a single government regulation, generated not only the need for a new automotive component (the catalytic converter), but also for other products needed in the manufacture of this component and for new kinds of fuels and their processes. But this was not all.

The imposition of standards invariably requires means to verify compliance. Emission inspection became mandatory and created market needs for computerized analytical equipment operable by the authorized inspection stations.

As of today, about fifty dollars worth of platinum is placed in each catalytic converter. Attempts have been made to decrease this cost by finding substitutes for platinum. So far success has been limited in the use of less expensive platinum metal group elements such as palladium.

The early catalytic converters now in use are beginning to reach the limit of their useful life. Therefore, because they contain appreciable values of recoverable platinum group metals, a new business has developed, concerning the collection and reclamation of used converters. The reclamation business has generated the need for equipment suitable for the processing of used converters, and for reagents used in such processing.

While the United States implemented this kind of environmental control, only few other nations followed the same path. In recent years, the European Community decided to impose similar emission standards. Market needs will be generated outside the United States, but they will not necessarily parallel the domestic history, because foreign cars have different engine sizes and designs.

An example of the repercussions of emission control in various regions of the western world is given in Figure 3.3, where gross platinum demand for automotive applications from 1976 to 1988 is graphically represented for North America, Japan, and the other regions (principally Europe).

What was learned with regard to the emission cleaning of the gasoline engine can be applied to the definition of the market needs that may arise if standards will be imposed on diesel engines. Of course, the specific needs and the products that will satisfy them will be different.

Market needs that derive from government regulations have a peculiar characteristic. The customers that are affected by such regulations are willing to collaborate with suppliers and regulating agencies whenever an industrially producible product leads to compliance. These customers, however, are very

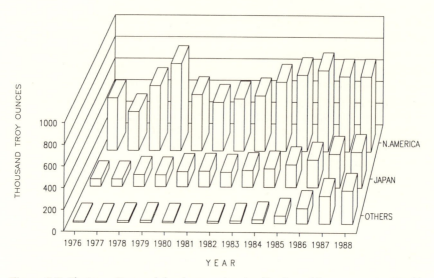

Figure 3.3 Platinum Demand for Automotive Applications, Noncommunist World, 1976–88

*Source*: Smith, F. John, Ed. *Platinum 1989*. London: Johnson Matthey Public Limited Company, 1989.

disturbed by the emergence of experimental products that may never be producible. The regulatory agencies usually base their standard on currently available technology; but the issue of industrial producibility may not be taken into consideration in defining available technology. Suppliers should exercise caution in surmising that their new product ideas will always be accepted by their potential customers, especially when the issue of industrial producibility has not been seriously considered.

### Telecommunication Networks

When Paul Revere hung a lantern in the North Church of Boston in 1775 to signal that the British were coming, he used a primitive, but effective, photonic telecommunication system. The signal travelled at the speed of light; thus, the message was received instantaneously. The functioning of that telecommunication network was identical to that of a modern fiber optic cable; the main difference was that, in a second, Paul Revere transmitted only a few bits of information ("They are coming by land," or "They are coming by sea") whereas, in the same time, modern optical fibers can transmit one hundred billion bits. A highly sophisticated contemporary system would have been no more effective than the colonial one, if the only function were to deliver the message that Paul Revere had in mind.

During the early years of the Industrial Revolution, telecommunication networks depended primarily on the telegraph, and the messages were transmitted as electrical impulses along a pair of copper wires. In the 1920s, voice communication (the telephone) began to grow rapidly and partially supplanted the telegraph. It was still based on copper line pairs, which, initially, could carry on only one conversation at a time. Advances in electronics increased the number of simultaneous conversation per line pair to 64; but not until the advent of fiber optic cables could the number of simultaneous communications be increased to several tens of thousand per fiber.

The initial experiments on fiber optic communications were carried out before the end of the nineteenth century by the inventor of the telephone, Alexander Graham Bell. His laboratory curiosity became a potential reality only after two new products were independently developed: optical fibers that could transmit light without losing much of its intensity, and light sources—the lasers—that could emit a very orderly kind of radiation. A technically feasible system was assembled only in 1970; but yet another technical development had to occur for this invention to become a major innovation, that is, to be widely commercialized: a practicable technique for splicing fiber optic cables in the field. Today, fiber optic telecommunication cables cross the oceans and span continents. They have become an everyday reality.

Fiber optic technology has invaded less than 10 percent of the telephone networks. Why is such a superior technology yet to be used extensively in the major portion of such network, connecting the subscribers to the telephone exchanges?

In long distance communications, the enormous capacity of fiber optic cables decreases the cost of communication per unit of information transmitted. Not so in the case of the individual subscribers, unless they require more than calling a relative or making a dinner reservation. Personal computers and telefaxing have increased the demand for communication from some residential and most commercial telephones, but yet, the copper line pair is adequate in this regard. Should the videophone take hold, or should shopping by mail in a customized fashion become a market need, copper line pair could be found inadequate and fiber optic cables could diffuse into the major portion of telephone networks. In short, success hinges primarily on changes in lifestyle and consumer preference.

Fiber optic connections to individual residential subscribers are likely to become a viable market target only in two circumstances; if a government intervention will mandate such event in anticipation of long-range societal benefits, and/or if the market needs will extend to many other functions, such as banking, security and safety monitoring, utility meter reading, movies at home by request, videophones, and others. One major telecommunication company is currently undertaking a pilot project at a California location to study the technical feasibility and market reaction of such comprehensive residential services via fiber optics networks. Time will tell whether high volume telecommunication service in residences is a real market need.

The new product developer who is depending on this plausible vision of the future should consider another factor. Today, a large number of households are connected to cable television networks, which have much higher communication capacities than telephone wires. These networks will compete with fiber optic cables supplied by the telephone operating companies. Whoever is visualizing an increased demand for two-way telecommunications from residences should be sensitive to the existence of this alternative network and, ideally, develop products that could serve either one.

## Conclusions

Market needs must be defined, at least qualitatively, before embarking in detailed product planning and applying substantial resources to new product development. The major emphasis should be on the functions required.

Needs are subjective, and therefore they cannot be determined by depending on a single source of information. Initially, a broad view of market needs must be obtained by consolidating and cross-examining the opinions derived from a variety of sources.

Market needs are dynamic. They should take into consideration potential changes in many areas, from technical, to political, to sociological.

A preliminary definition of the new products sought at the earliest possible time is desirable and often essential. Product definition need not be precise in the early stage of product planning, but must be comprehensive in its principal components.

### Note

1. George F. Sharrard, "Understanding the Environment of New Business Ventures." In *Successful Product and Business Development*, edited by Newman H. Giragosian (New York, New York: Marcel Dekker, 1978), 99–114.

# 4

## Sources of New Product Ideas

### Introduction

Ideas for new products are primarily the result of market needs, but once these ideas are developed, they constitute only a framework onto which more specific product ideas must be defined.

Should we generate a very large number of potential ideas in order to maximize the probability of finding, among them, a few that are outstanding? Certain theories suggest that this is indeed the case. The human mind seldom works on a straight line; it makes progress by trial and error. Thus, it is unwise to restrict creative thinking to a single, well-defined objective. Moreover, creative endeavors should be divorced from the critical analysis of the ideas they generate. These concepts constitute the foundations of several creative session techniques.

The generation of a large number of new product ideas has its drawbacks. When confronted with a challenging goal, the human mind becomes very productive. At the same time the mind tends to release the pressure by creating trivial answers. Thus the urge to generate a very large number of new product ideas in order to find, among them, some that are likely to lead to technical and commercial success may result in the generation of a wish list rather than a sound portfolio of alternative choices.

As an example, a manufacturer that deals only with commodity products wants to diversify into specialty and value-added new products. According to the product integration flowsheet that was previously mentioned (see Chapter 1), the number of opportunities vastly expands as one moves from a basic commodity (say, an industrial organic chemical such as ethylene) to specialty and fabricated products (such as resins and their derivative engineered plastic components). Searching for new product ideas, that manufacturer may proceed too far along the product integration tree and consider many consumer needs that are satisfied by plastic components. The possibilities are so numerous that only a wish list would originate from such creative exercise. By narrowing the limits of the search, the exercise is likely to become more productive without unduly impairing creativity.

The ultimate goal of new product development is to strengthen a company's position in the market by improving its product portfolio. Hence it makes little difference whether a product that is new for that company never existed before, existed but was never commercialized previously, or was an article of commerce not marketed by that company, as long as the ultimate business objective is fulfilled. The definition of new product development must, therefore, be extended to the adoption, acquisition, modification, and commercialization of preexisting products.

Today many business opportunities are based on ownership transfers. Many products that are unprofitable in a given environment may become excellent performers in a different environment.

Consistent with this expanded definition, the search for ideas must comprehend the external world as well as the internal confine. The latter is most productive if comprising individuals and organizational units that are frequently in contact with the outer world.

## External Sources of New Product Ideas

### The Incubators

European business enterprises have long profited from central organizations (consisting of centers of excellence in specialized technological fields) that may be independent, or may be branches of universities. These organizations are usually supported jointly by the public and private sectors and receive a strong input from educational institutions (which are often public). The triad government-industry-university is, therefore, a strong foundation for business. This has been possible outside the United States because government intervention and guidance were more readily accepted than domestically; also because antitrust regulations have been less restrictive and sometimes not existent in comparison with those of the United States.

In the United States, the beneficial action of that triad has been a more recent phenomenon. We have seen the creation of many centers of excellence, and the emergence of "incubators." These are multi-supported organizations that flesh out raw ideas at least until they attract the attention and support of for-profit enterprises. At the same time, part of the resources that the private sector used to devote to internal research and development have been progressively shifted to the partial support of centralized institutions.

### The Matchmakers

Matchmakers are of two kinds. Some facilitate the encounter of organizations or individuals that have developed new products with those that may have an interest in commercializing them after acquiring proprietary rights. Others facilitate the encounter of organizations that have needs with others that may be in a position of satisfying such needs by developing new products. Both are excellent sources of new product ideas.

The first type of matchmaker has been in operation for a long time. For instance, the National Aeronautics and Space Administration (NASA) has an outstanding mechanism for technology transfer.[1] Ten Field Centers have technology utilization officers who manage center participation in these activities; ten Industrial Application Centers offer information retrieval and other assistance to users; and 37 Industrial Application Center Affiliates further facilitate transfer. In addition, the Computer Software Management and Information Center (COSMIC) offers government-developed software for secondary use. So far, more than 30,000 secondary applications have derived from NASA-developed technology, many in the health, public safety, environmental, and manufacturing technology areas.

The Department of Defense has not followed this route until very recent time. Today, the transfer of technologies developed for military purposes to the private sector is an official policy.[2]

Similar programs aimed at searching for buyers of inventions have been operated in the private sector.

Consulting firms often act as matchmakers, either on a spot basis (that is, whenever a client they serve for other reasons happens to have something for sale or wants to acquire something), or in a systematic way. Sometimes, they get part of their reward as a minor equity in whatever new enterprise originates.

A different kind of matchmaker advertises needs and seeks products and ideas. One of the most successful programs of this kind is the Small Business Innovation Research (SBIR) operated by the U.S. government. After realizing that small enterprises have been, on balance, more creative than large organizations, the U.S. government set aside a percentage of its R&D contract funds for small business (as defined by the Small Business Administration) and simplified the procedures for proposal submission (since a small business can hardly afford the elaborate procedure that prevails in most government R&D contract proposals).

The SBIR program originates a number of solicitation brochures describing the new product needs of various government organizations in more or less specific terms.[3] The bidder has an opportunity to obtain modest funds to prove an innovating concept. If it obtains an award and succeeds in proving a new concept, it may bid for more funds in order to develop the concept into a product. If this second phase is successful, it may obtain substantial funds to makes this invention industrially producible. In this case, it must identify a larger enterprise, willing to bring at least some intangible contribution to this endeavor.

After this program was established, others, operated in the private sector, emerged. One of these[4] is carried out by Advanced Technology Innovations, Inc. (ATI). This service is free to the potential inventors and supported by large companies who advertise, through ATI, their needs. Potential inventors respond to a description of need by submitting to ATI a nonconfidential version of their ideas and approaches. If accepted, inventor and sponsoring large companies negotiate directly and privately as they see fit. Requests span vast technological areas; for instance, novel ways of desulfurizing natural gas, flame retardant, secure and reusable software components, and specialized instrumentation.

Participation in programs of this sort, be they publicly or privately sponsored, is valuable for both small and large enterprises. These programs are very stimulating for new product idea generation, even beyond their immediate scopes.

## New Products by Acquisition of Companies

A business enterprise may adopt a new product by acquiring a company or a company operation. These acquisitions usually include proprietary rights on current and potentially new products that the acquired operation has developed. The acquired company also brings to the acquiring company a capability for new product development and several embryonic new product ideas.

The shedding of operations that no longer fit, especially in very large corporations that derived from the merger of several forerunners, is a very common occurrence. Certain operations have changed hands more than once in a single year.

The company that is seeking new products is well advised to explore these possibilities. One approach is to identify its competitors and see which one, or ones, belong to incongruous environments. Especially when these environments have been recently created by acquisitions of mergers, the probability that these competitive operations may, some day, be shed by the parent corporation is significant. If they are relatively small, and therefore do not generate antitrust issues, they should be analyzed further with regard to their developmental products and their potential to generate new product ideas. This is no simple task; but its rewards are handsome, especially if the new products sought are substantially different than those of the acquiring company.

## The Revival of Obsolete Products

Some obsolete products are like the mythological Phoenix—they are born again from their ashes—often because of extraneous events. The oil embargo of 1973, for instance, gave coal and wood burning stoves a second chance. The U.S. Census of Manufacturers reported shipments of 326,000 units in 1967, decreasing to 228,000 in 1972, and then sharply increasing to 1,062,000 in 1977 and 1,114,000 in 1982.

Initially the market drive was energy saving. Manufacturers endeavored to improve obsolete versions of wood burning stoves from several points of view besides increased thermal efficiency. Attention was paid to aesthetic features; maintenance was simplified; some models were designed so that they could be integrated with modern fireplaces. The acceptance of these heating appliances was substantial; but soon problems were encountered, mainly concerning creosote coating of flues and attendant fire hazard. This problem generated the need for a new product—a catalytic unit that destroys some of the undesirable emissions while further improving thermal efficiency. The old Franklin stove was transformed into a high technology article.

### Customers and Competitors

Customers are the most obvious sources of new product ideas. This includes current customers, potential customers served by others, and those that constitute new markets created by the new products. As an example, the facsimile machine that is so popular today has created a new market niche, probably unsuspected by the original developers. We now see these machines used by small grocers and fast food operators for receiving orders from their customers. The use of facsimile avoids the continuous interruptions created by the ringing phone, so more disruptive in peak times, when the personnel are busy filling previous orders. It avoids errors due to misunderstanding created in verbal communications—more frequent when the helpers do not have a good command of the English language. Facsimiles constitute a positive proof that an order was given, and are therefore useful in the rare cases when the orders are not picked up. Where else could they find specific niches? Could they be adapted or improved for other applications?

New product ideas originating from direct customers are consistent with market needs; therefore, what was mentioned in the previous chapter is also valid here. These ideas should be formulated by considering a cross section of opinions, rather than a single input. They should be reviewed and revised because market needs are dynamic.

The suggestion that new product ideas could originate from competitors may appear surprising. Yet, "me too" products are often viable, given ways to negotiate licensing agreements or other arrangements if proprietary rights are involved. A competitor's product may also stimulate thinking about a better way to serve the customers. There are, after all *bad* products on the market, and they constitute excellent points of departure for the development of better ideas. Finally, it is not unusual to have situations where cross-licensing can benefit both parties, and others where joint venture R&D, once mainly limited to non-competitors seeking the development of risky new ventures, are appropriate.

## Internal Sources of Ideas

Every organizational sector can effectively contribute to the generation of new product ideas, each from its own viewpoint. The melding of these diversified inputs is the most effective way to ensure a thorough and sensible outcome. In theory, this methodology is very sound. In practice it is very difficult to reduce to practice, especially in large and complex establishments. The difficulties arise from several sources. First of all, those primarily responsible for new product development, be they in the technical, planning, or marketing organization, are reluctant to give any proposer of a new idea his day in court. Most ideas look plausible on the surface. Their analysis is a time-consuming endeavor and often results in substantial doubts about worthiness and viability. Even in the absence of the so-called *Not Invented Here* complex—the impulsive negative reaction to a suggestion that originates outside an organizational unit—new product developers have a hard time coping with an indiscriminate bombardment of suggestions. So much more, when the suggestions originate from higher levels of management.

A certain happy medium must be reached between indiscriminate acceptance of all suggestions and total exclusion of unrequested input, so that creativity is not impaired while some resemblance of order is maintained in the new product development organization.

The inclusion of detached personnel—that is, those not intimately involved with the specific task at hand, but otherwise competent and responsible—is highly desirable. Most effective are technical and business managers involved in other projects. They commonly love to withdraw briefly from their exacting responsibilities and let their experience, knowledge, and imagination help another project. Their involvement is, at times, most effective *because* (rather than in spite) of the fact that they have little time to answer questions extraneous to their operation. This sort of gentle pressure often stimulates imagination without causing anxiety.

Another kind of contributor to new product ideas may be found, at times, in the comptroller department. Comptrollers and their staff, if effective, have a good grasp of both operations and marketing. They are not involved, however, in specific projects and have an adequate, but superficial, knowledge of what is possible. At times their suggestions are promptly rejected, based on technical considerations; but often, they are found viable, or at least useful, as a point of departure.

Paraprofessional personnel must be listed as a prime source of new product ideas. All too often they are seldom included in creative sessions or even considered qualified to make suggestions. Their viewpoint is usually free from the negativism arising from deep knowledge of scientific principles. (After all, once upon a time, the principle of conservation of matter was an absolute scientific truth, and negated the idea that matter could be transformed into energy.) They have a strong motivation to graduate from their supporting function and to have a stronger voice in the direction of programs. They also have a very keen sense for what is practicable. Finally, they can often communicate with the outside world effectively and elicit less resistance in this respect than professionals and their managers.

Individuals who fit up to a point are present in every organization. They are loyal to their employers, but also somewhat detached. They usually have a strong independent spirit, are opinionated, and often are gifted in terms of creativity. These individuals often become the repository of a special kind of knowledge that becomes very useful when the principal task is to develop new product ideas. In management science literature they have been called "gate-keepers," but this appellative is perhaps too restrictive. Yes, they hold the keys to many gates, both in technology and marketing, but after all they are individuals *par excellance* and it is their personality, more than their knowledge or role in the organization, that renders them so effective in new product idea generation.

The last internal source of new product ideas to be mentioned is the revival of discarded ideas. Some organizations have the habit of maintaining an ever-green list of ideas, from which some are extracted and further developed or used as a starting point for new projects. These eternal lists have the habit of degenerating with time and eventually deteriorating. The periodic rehashing of these lists often results in a frustrating experience. It may, however, be possible to find, among obsolete ideas, some that may be revived. The revival is more probable if it is made feasible by changes in the external environment. These lists should be used with discretion.

## Techniques for Creative Sessions

Is creativity an innate trait? Can it be measured? How can it be stimulated?

Notwithstanding many excellent research investigations on this subject, only some generic answers can be given to these questions. Obviously, not all individuals are fountainheads of new ideas; but some could potentially be so, given adequate encouragement and motivation. We seldom encounter individuals who are not creative at least in one particular aspect of their lives; but we see many who do not show creativity in the confines of their work assignments. Psychological tests that attempt to measure creativity are, therefore, of limited, and often of questionable, utility in the selection of the personnel who are likely to contribute effectively to new product ideas.

Motivation and environment are much more important, in this context, than innate ability. Motivation can be stimulated in many ways. One of the most popular is the establishment of some specific tangible reward for meritorious ideas and/or a public recognition. Though desirable, the effectiveness of these practices is usually limited.

The creation of an appropriate environment is a more powerful approach, and is under the control of the responsible executives who desire the generation of new product ideas. The environment should be nonthreatening, but should also induce some mild irritation or pressure. The environment should not censure those who "say the wrong thing," such as suggesting ideas that are obviously nonviable or making derogatory remarks on company products. For these reasons, in large and complex enterprises creative sessions that include several levels of management are often ineffective. However, in tightly knit, small companies that have only two or three levels of management creativity is not impaired in similar circumstances.

Environment has to do also with the physical surroundings during the creative session. Nothing is more damaging than interruptions, whether caused by a telephone ringing, by a messenger, or by the coming and going of busy executives. Any quiet room, exclusively devoted to the creative session, would do the job; but, in certain cases, it is desirable to move off work premises. Here too there is a happy medium. A creative session held at a resort may comprise an environment that is too relaxing and distracting.

A certain amount of pressure is productive. To establish a relatively short time limit is the simplest way to exercise such pressure. If more time is needed, creative sessions could be resumed later, or scheduled in two sections, not too far apart in time.

There are several techniques to stimulate creative thinking and several consulting firms that can assist those who are seeking new product ideas. One such firm is Synectics, Inc. Initially, this firm depended on the concept that creation consists of making new connections between seemingly unrelated items. The new connections are easier to establish if old connections are first destroyed, because the knowledge that we have accumulated through study and experience oftentimes has an inhibiting influence.

In his paper reciting the history of Synectics,® Prince[5] lists, among others, the following actions that discourage or encourage creativity:

Actions that Discourage Creativity:
   Be pessimistic, judgmental, critical.
   Be impatient, nitpicking, disruptive.
   Blame, ridicule, call names.
   Dominate, order, threaten, demand.
   Put burden of proof on others, cross-examine.
   Be cynical, negative, insist on early precision.
   Be inattentive, act distant, silent.

Actions that Encourage Creativity:
   Listen attentively, acknowledge, give early support.
   Eliminate status, deal as equals.
   Take responsibility for understanding.
   Speculate, be open, build on others' ideas.
   Protect vulnerable beginning.
   Share the burden of the proof.
   Support uncertainty and confusion, use ambiguity.

Over the years, Synectics extended its endeavors to facets of the new product development process that are beyond the idea generation. Its New Product

Commitment™ program, for instance, includes business analysis, integration with company objectives, testing, and commercialization.

Whatever technique one selects to use, the presence of a facilitator is highly desirable. The facilitator can be a consultant, an employee who is regarded as nonthreatening by the members of the creative session, or a leader selected by consensus among the participants.

Creative sessions should be held periodically. They are helpful in making participants comfortable with this type of exercise, and to refine participants' skills in this regard. They should not be very time consuming. They should not be undertaken only to attack very important issues. The skills developed in organizing a company outing are transferable to the development of new product ideas.

## Examples

Two examples are given to further expound on concepts and suggestions described above. *Aurora* gives a brief history of a collaborative government-industry-university project that yielded a new commercial product for the industrial participant. *SBIR* describes details of the U.S. Government operation that is instrumental in harnessing the inventive power of small businesses.

### Aurora

Aurora™ is the trade mark of audiometric equipment manufactured and marketed by Nicolet Instrument Corp., a public corporation producing instruments for industrial and medical applications. Corporate revenues are currently on the order of 150 million dollars per year. This audiodiagnostic instrument derived from a collaborative endeavor of Project Phoenix, Inc. of Madison, Wisconsin.[6] The participants were Nicolet, the Wisconsin Alumni Research Foundation, the University of Wisconsin, and the Wisconsin Department of Development.

The original idea was generated in the university environment and motivated by the desire to help the hearing impaired by creating a hearing aid free from many of the drawbacks of state-of-the-art items, and capable of being customized for each individual. In order to develop this new product, it was necessary first to develop a sophisticated audiodiagnostic instrument. Such an instrument needed much flexibility of testing, and the capability of storing and manipulating large amounts of clinical data.

The technical development of the project was carried out both at the University of Wisconsin campus and on Nicolet's premises with substantial industrial financial support. The resulting product consisted of sophisticated hardware (including an IBM-AT processor), operated by powerful software specifically designed for audiological testing and hearing aid fitting.

After extensive testing, this instrument was commercialized. At the same time, the development of a digital, programmable hearing aid was carried out.[7] The latter development was dependent upon the audiodiagnostic instrument, because other instruments were regarded deficient in generating detailed information on the patient's hearing conditions and hearing aid preferences.

This success story exemplifies one way of translating a well-defined market need to one or more product ideas aimed at satisfying such a need. The collaborative route was, in this case, more effective than the development by an individual company would have been. The project succeeded not only in moving speedily toward the goal, but also in creating a center of excellence that is likely to pay handsome dividends in the long run.

## SBIR

The Small Business Innovation Research program (SBIR) is administered by several sponsoring agencies, but has a unifying procedure. The ultimate goal is to exploit the traditional inventiveness of small businesses, and to promote technology transfer from these businesses to larger organizations.

The mechanics of this program consist of the following steps. The U.S. Small Business Administration disseminates among small businesses periodic pre-solicitation announcements. These warn the readers about forthcoming requests for proposals by several agencies. These agencies include the Departments of Agriculture, Commerce, Defense, Education, Energy, Health and Human Services, Transportation, the Environmental Protection Agency, NASA, the National Science Foundation, and the Nuclear Regulatory Agency. The pre-solicitation announcements indicate the subjects of interest, the date the solicitations will be issued, when the proposals are due, and the addresses of the sponsoring organizations.

Here are examples of new product needs mentioned in pre-solicitation announcements:

- Food and Drug Administration: Computer system to model metabolic pathways of specific toxic chemicals.
- Federal Aviation Administration: Advanced deicing fluids for general aviation aircrafts.
- Federal Highway Administration: Shear stress gauge for hydraulic laboratory use.
- United States Coast Guard: Remote site power by wave energy.
- Department of Health and Human Services: Improved industrial hand tools to prevent musculoskeletal impairment.
- Department of the Navy: Clothing system for static electricity control.
- Defense Advanced Research Projects Agency: Low-cost hydrophone technology.

Each sponsoring organization periodically issues program solicitations that describe the needs of the sponsor. They also include a description of the procedure for submitting proposals, and the indication of where additional information or help can be obtained. The procedure for submitting proposals is streamlined in order not to excessively burden the small businesses.

New proposers must bid for a Phase I program, typically a $50,000 research lasting six months, aimed at proving novel concepts. Preference is given to credible, but risky, approaches to the solution of complex and difficult problems. All proposals are kept confidential, but, if a bidder wins an award, an abstract of his proposal is published.

Such abstracts are exceedingly useful for *large* businesses as well, if they are seeking new product ideas and technology transfer. A large business can, at this point, contact the small business and indicate interest in participating later in this project.

Those companies that successfully complete Phase I, may submit a proposal for Phase II—a more substantial endeavor, typically funded at $250,000 and lasting some two years. In Phase II the participation of a collaborating large business is desirable, but not mandatory. Phase II must prove the viability of a new product or process, and project the way such technology could be commercialized.

Successfully completed Phase II projects give the proposer the privilege of submitting a substantial Phase III proposal, aimed at demonstrating industrial producibility. In this case, a large business must participate and contribute support, whether directly or indirectly.

The SBIR program has been very successful, and funds thereof have been utilized very efficiently. As a by-product, the proposal solicitations have created a readily accessible set of definitions of market needs. The scopes of these proposals span a very wide range of subjects and ultimate objectives.

Here is an example, taken from a solicitation by the Department of Energy. The market need is defined by the desire to save energy in the top floor of buildings by utilizing daylight. The product sought is an unconventional roof structure (conventional skylights are explicitly excluded) incorporating daylight apertures and related controls. The design must integrate such apertures with heating and ventilating system, electric lighting, and electrical distribution. The proposal continues by describing specific features sought, desirable materials of constructions, and other details.

## Conclusions

Sources of new product ideas primarily originate from the definition of market needs. However, they seldom originate directly from current or potential customers.

New product ideas should include not only ideas on products that can be developed from within, but also those that can be acquired through licensing, joint ventures, or by acquiring other concerns. Collaborative arrangements are very effective in generating new product ideas. Among these, the "incubators"—generally consortia of industries, universities, and government—have been very valuable.

Internally, new product ideas should be elicited in all organizational sectors; but caution should be exercised in this regard, lest those who are directly responsible for new product development spend excessive energy in evaluating what is put in the suggestion box.

Some individuals in each organization are especially gifted in idea generation; but all persons can give meaningful contributions, when properly motivated.

The environment in which new product idea generation occurs must be conducive, and participants should not be exposed to criticism or anxieties. A certain pressure, however, is generally beneficial to creative thinking.

There are several techniques for stimulating idea generation. There are several organizations that help in this regard. Among these, the Small Business Innovation Research program has been very successful and can help significantly both small and large businesses.

## Notes

1. James J. Haggerty, *Spinoff 1988*, National Aeronautics and Space Administration, Office of Commercial Programs Technology Utilization Division (Washington, DC: U.S. Government Printing Office, August 1988).

2. United States, Federal Technology Transfer Act of 1986. Public Law 99-502, October 20, 1986.

3. The Small Business Administration, Office of Innovation Research and Technology, Washington, DC, periodically issues *Pre-Solicitation Announcements*. These publications contain the names and addresses of all government departments and agencies that participate in the SBIR program. Each department or agency issue *Program Solicitations*. These documents are sent to interested parties upon request.

4. Technology Innovation Program™, *Program Solicitation* (Tyson's Corner, Virginia: Advanced Technology Innovations, Inc.). Issued periodically.

5. George M. Prince, "Synectics: Twenty-Five Years of Research into Creativity and Group Process," *Training and Development Journal*, 201 (1982): 76–79.

6. Nicolet Instrument Corporation, "A Comprehensive Instrument for Clinical Audiology and Hearing Aid Fitting." *Hearing Instruments*, 38, no. 1 (1987): 37–38, 64.

7. Ross J. Roeser and Kenya Taylor, "Audiometric and Field Testing with a Digital Hearing Instrument." *Hearing Instruments*, 39, no.4 (1988): 14–16, 18, 20, 22.

# 5

## Marketing Research

### Introduction

Is there a difference between *market* and *marketing* research? According to prevailing semantics, market denotes a state of affairs outside the selling organization whereas marketing denotes such state of affairs plus the interactions between sellers and buyers. The term marketing research is preferred because it is more comprehensive and leads to the establishment of a data base useful not only for the planning, but also for the implementation of new projects. Marketing research is here defined as those activities that generate quantitative information on market needs and on the most desirable modes to satisfy such needs through the development and distribution of new products.

As an example, a toy manufacturer determined that the market needs an interactive videotape product that gives the user the option of selecting one of several choices. Marketing research quantifies this market need in terms of anticipated sales per year, price sensitivity, subject matter, etc. It also defines the most appropriate distribution channels (toy store? audio/video tape store? direct sales?) and the marketing dynamics (anticipated rate of penetration, effect of initial pricing, discount policies, etc.).

In the previous chapter the qualitative definition of market needs was emphasized as the most desirable *initial* approach to new product development, noting that such definition must eventually be quantified. To which extent is such quantification necessary or desirable? Quantification can be extended to the finest segmentations in terms of region, buyers, product line options, and other criteria, or can be limited to an approximate assessment of total market size. Where should one stop in refining quantitative information? The answer is product-specific and depends on the business environment.

Generally the approximate assessment of the total market size is a desirable first step, because, at times, it may be sufficient to decide to *abandon* a project. It is never sufficient to decide to *pursue* a project because many other factors must be considered in order to assess the probability of success. After establishing an adequate initial data base, further refinement can safely be delayed to later stages of the new product development process. These successive reiterations of marketing research are usually essential.

How reliable are market data? It depends on several factors, the most important being the understanding of what the data mean. For example, a mining company wonders whether it should enter the indium business, in view of recent technical developments in the electronic industries that may increase the demand for this metal. This company reads in a financial periodical the conclusions of a consulting company report that projects a threefold increase in indium demand in the next ten years. What does this information mean? Does the report refer to values or quantities? To total indium consumed, including recycling, or to primary indium only? Of electronic grade only or also of metallurgical, lower purity grade? Do the data concern the United States, the western world, or the entire world?

Inadequate reliability of marketing data bases may depend on faulty data bases and/or biases. A data base is often faulty because it rides on another data base that is faulty. For instance, we learn that the intensity of use of a certain product (defined as the use of such product per unit gross national product) is higher in country X than in country Y. This comparison is unreliable when the gross national product data are faulty—a common occurrence in those countries where a substantial fraction of the economy is not reported in the official statistics (the so-called underground economy). More generally, caution should be exercised when the data base is expressed in terms of *relative* values, or ranking, without revealing sources that contain the underlying *absolute* values.

All data bases are affected by bias. For instance, projections of future markets for a given product, originating from a buyer and a seller are likely to be biased in opposite directions. The buyer is likely to be optimistic about the future of a product that he needs, because such attitude promotes competition, increases supplies, and puts downward pressure on prices. A dominant seller is likely to be pessimistic in order to discourage competition. Data bases, therefore, should not be merely accepted. They should be scrutinized and interpreted.

Another example. Projections of peak demand for electrical energy in the United States were overestimated. Specifically, the 1984 summer peak demand estimated in 1977 was 30 percent higher than the actual demand.[1] Projections essentially underestimated the effects of the conservation drives caused primarily by the sharp increase in energy price.

Whenever biases cannot be analyzed and corrected, they can be alleviated by comparing several independent data bases and developing a reasonable consensus.

One of the worst difficulties concerning data bases is the self-perpetuation of faulty data. Primary data (say, statistics generated and published by an agency of the Department of Commerce or Interior) are quoted, and often manipulated, by consulting firms, magazine editors, authors of topical books, and students working on their dissertations. These secondary sources are then quoted by another source, and so on. These derived data may be eventually included in a computerized information file which can be easily retrieved and therefore is used frequently. In these cases, the primary sources are seldom identified. Therefore, it is not unusual to acquire a data base that can be traced to the original source only after a time-consuming effort. This state of affairs is disturbing even if errors are not introduced in these transfers, and if the meaning of the data (for instance, the unit) are not misquoted or omitted—events that compound problems.

## Why Marketing Research?

There are three fundamental reasons for undertaking marketing research. The first, and most important, is to reduce business risk. This is, after all, the main reason for doing any research. The more one knows, the better one can assess risks.

Research, including marketing research, is not essential. One could produce a new product, bring it to market, and see whether it sells. If the effort to develop the product and the cost of manufacturing it are low, this may be the most cost-effective approach. After all the ultimate way of conducting marketing research is to market!

In the context of industrial new product development, this approach would obviously be suicidal. Development and manufacturing costs are always substantial. Therefore, the second reason for undertaking marketing research is to guide technical development. Marketing research helps to define the new product in a variety of ways, and especially with regard to its functional specifications and to its differentiation from competitive products.

To establish a base for commercial development is the third reason for undertaking marketing research. The new product, if successful, will be advertised and taken to market. These endeavors are greatly helped by a quantitative understanding of market needs, distribution channels, price sensitivity, and other factors that often can be estimated a priori.

At times, marketing research induces to discontinue the development of products that are unlikely to be successful, thereby optimizing the utilization of available resources.

## Sources of Market Data

Market data can be historical or projected. Contrary to common belief, significant and reliable market data are not easy to retrieve and are sometimes unavailable. Difficulties are more severe now because most markets are global and often involve the less developed countries. Changes in life-style constitute a principal difficulty when projections are made.

Domestically, there are many sources of market data, most of which are reasonably reliable. Cost containment in the federal government has led to a deterioration of several data bases. Others have deteriorated because the total volume of information has increased and therefore, given limited resources, the data generated have become more aggregated. Other data bases have become less meaningful because the segment that is usually called "Not Elsewhere Classified" has become a significant percentage of the total.

In other cases, market data are limited because products cannot be traced all the way to the ultimate users. This is often the case for commodity products. For instance, the shipments of various aluminum mill products from United States producers is known in terms of general application areas such as building, transportation, consumer durable, machinery, and containers. Further segmentation of certain application areas is more difficult or impossible to be determined. For instance, in the case of the transportation area, it may be desirable to know how much aluminum is used in passenger cars, for which components, and what fraction of these vehicles are exported.

One difficulty with market data derives from the international trade. For instance, the manufacturers of complex systems often outsource components abroad, rather than manufacturing them or buying them from domestic sources. In these cases, there is no direct correlation between the demand of the ultimate product, say, a passenger vehicle, and the demand of certain components or materials used in that product.

Take the case of a television set. We know how many sets are produced in the United States, and how many are imported. If the market research concerns television tubes, there is no direct relation between sets and tube produced or internationally traded. Much more complex is the case of the amount of glass consumed to produce the tubes.

Difficulties and complexity are multiplied when searching for marketing data in regions other than North America. Such difficulties depend on the specific region. Japan has many superb and very reliable market statistics; Western Europe is much more erratic; centrally planned economies are affected by low reliability; less developed countries—very important especially in the case of the neo-industrial countries—have hardly the resources to collect information and, at times, are reluctant to reveal what they know.

If marketing research is limited to the United States, the most desirable starting point is to become familiar with the Standard Industrial Classification (SIC) system.[2] This system divides products according to a cascading classification. The most aggregated category is designated by a two-digit code; the next by a three-digit, and so on. For instance, in the SIC code 38 signifies instruments, watches, medical and optical goods, etc., 381 certain kinds of instruments, 3811 engineering and scientific instruments, 38111 aeronautical, nautical, and navigational instruments not sending or receiving radio controls, and 38111 08 altimeters (except radio and radar). The sum of the totals of disaggregated classifications (e.g., the sum of 38111, 38112, etc) constitutes the total of the next level of classification (e.g., 3811) and so on.

The SIC code has limitations. Invariably, certain products of interest appear only in classifications that are excessively aggregated. Nevertheless, it is very useful to trace marketing data because most government statistics and many publications from the private sector, such as regional or national list of manufacturers, follow this system.

For developers who want to become oriented in a market area with which they are unfamiliar, a good starting point is to peruse *U.S. Industrial Outlook*.[3] This yearly publication gives a general description of the principal two-digit SIC code areas, reports selected statistics and their sources, and gives at least qualitative projections. Some areas are further subdivided into their component elements.

The next step in tracing market data is to peruse the *Current Industrial Reports*,[4] published periodically (some monthly). In major cities, the Bureau of the Census maintains an office open to the public which assists in the search and has a full set of reports available for inspection. These offices also advise about specialists in Washington who may assist further with the interpretation of data or additional data. In order to use this information source effectively, it is essentially to determine first the SIC codes of interest.

The most comprehensive, but complex, data base is the *Census of Manufactures*,[5] a monumental periodic publication. At times, marketing data must be derived indirectly, or sorted out among a large number of other information.

The major limitations of these sources are two: certain data are not available because either they have not been collected, or because their publication would reveal proprietary information (this is the case, for instance, when the concentration of manufacturers is high), and data are always reported in terms of values but only erratically in terms of quantities. For instance, in the case of altimeters (SIC 38111 08) we know that in 1977, product shipments amounted to about 20 million dollars, but we do not know how many units were shipped.

Other U.S. government departments (e.g., Transportation, Energy) publish statistics that are useful for marketing research. However, the most useful data derive from trade associations, or consulting firms working independently or in conjunction with a trade association.

Most developers are familiar with their own trade associations and trade journals. Should they want to explore product lines with which they are unfamiliar, they can become acquainted with the pertinent trade association by perusing one of the available directories. As an example, the *Encyclopedia of Associations*[6] lists many associations that can be useful for tracing market data.

Many consulting firms are excellent sources of marketing data. Some firms publish proprietary reports that are available for a fixed price; others may be operating only on a multiclient or single client basis. The search for appropriate consulting firms can be carried out by referral (often by a trade association), or by perusing one of the published directories. As an example, *Dun's Consultant Directory*®[7] is one such source.

## Timing of New Product Introduction

Successes and failures are often a function of timing more than other factors. Many products were introduced prematurely; the market was not ready to accept them as yet. Pioneers wasted precious resources, whereas followers capitalized on the pioneers' wrong timing. The personal computer is a case in point. When first introduced, such a powerful appliance was regarded by many users as an overwhelming and almost forbidding machine. It was approached with timidity. The pioneers eventually reaped handsome benefits by modifying their products and promoting the development of user-friendly software. Many followers, on the other hand, reached almost instant success without applying large resources to development.

Another example is the early failure of interactive marketing services offered by cable television. Rather primitive, these services allowed a subscriber to send by telephone a code that directed the producer to telecast a specific advertisement chosen from a preset list. This service was discontinued after a while for lack of tangible payoff. Undoubtedly, interactive services of this kind will return in much more sophisticated versions, and will be accepted by the consumers, but in this case timing was premature.

Timing is critical also in the case of marketing research, if for no other reason than market needs are dynamic. If carried out too early, it is likely to yield a picture of what the market was like at the beginning of the development rather than at the end and beyond. This issue is much more severe the longer the lead time needed for technical and market development.

Timing is also critical because, in the earliest stages of new product development, the developer does not know which questions to ask, but to delay marketing research until the new product has been developed will invariably result in a waste of effort, unless such product is but an improvement of what the developer is already marketing successfully.

If too early and too late are undesirable, where does the happy medium lie? There is no happy medium. Marketing research must be a continuing and reiterative activity, initially superficial but extensive; then, in subsequent reiterations, progressively more profound but focused.

## Mechanisms of Marketing Research

Confronted with the need to conduct marketing research on a new product or product idea, the developer is likely to ask the question: should I do it in-house or should I farm it out? The answer is invariably neither.

In-house marketing research is implemented effectively for products and markets with which the developer is already familiar. Particularly in the case of new products for diversification, adequate in-house know-how is unlikely to exist.

Even if the know-how is adequate, in-house activities are likely to be somewhat biased, and not necessarily in the optimistic direction. A company may, for instance, be affected by prior failures and be too conservative in the assessment of new market potentials. Internal politics may play roles that bias the results, or the interpretation of the results. More generally, in-house activities, even if sound and thorough, are unlikely to search for fatal flaws.

Case in point: a leading supplier of polyethylene planned to develop an engineered component aimed at promoting the use of polyethylene at the expense of one of several metals. In-house marketing research determined that the demand for that component was on a growth trend; thus, the component manufacturers had an opportunity to design new plants that could take advantage of lower overall costs caused by the use of polyethylene. The project was implemented, achieved technical success, but was a commercial failure. Potential customers decided not to change their manufacturing methods because they would have become dependent on a single raw material rather than several metals competing with each other. In-house marketing research failed to uncover this hidden killer.

Farmed-out marketing research may consist of purchasing a proprietary report and interpreting its results. At times, such purchase also entitles the buyer to a limited amount of direct consultation. Alternatively, marketing research can be contracted on a custom basis, in which case the results are proprietary to the client. The first route is often the most expedient and economical. The report may, however, contain non-pertinent information and lack specific critical details. The report could be regarded as a first step and supplemented by in-house, or custom, research.

The hiring of a consulting firm for a specific, customized research is by far the most effective route, but it is costly and is generally of limited effectiveness unless consultant and client establish first a sound rapport. A company that wants to commission such research should identify more than one qualified consultant, meet with each one, describe in very specific terms what it wants to learn, obtain references, assess track records, and then carefully review the proposals received. Once a proposal is accepted, a principal liaison person should be appointed and utilized for most communications; interim reviews should be scheduled; guidance should be given to the remaining portion of the study. Better still, the research could be carried out collaboratively, at a time with a client's representative stationed temporarily on the consultant's premises.

When the importance of the task at hand warrants it, the developer may want to hire more than one consultant and compare their results. Each consultant is then asked to further justify those results that are not consistent with the common consensus.

In all cases, farmed-out marketing research should be scrutinized with regard to several factors. These must include: sources of data (published, based on telephone interviews, based on personal interviews, derived from consultant's proprietary files, etc.), methodology used in manipulating historical data and in making projections, and logics on which all conclusions and recommendations are based.

Whether carried out in-house, farmed-out, or done collaboratively, marketing research should lead to the following information:

- Quantitative market assessment: historical, current, and projected. Time span of projections depend on product life and other factors. For long-life products, three and ten years are reasonable targets. For short-life products, one and five years. Projections beyond ten years are usually of limited value because of market dynamics.
- Competitive analysis: product and industry. Functional and direct competition between existing and new products should be analyzed. The structures of the industries manufacturing all competitive products should be understood, in terms of constitution, size, financial strength, and other pertinent features.
- Environment: financial, regulatory, and social. Consideration should be given to financial issues such as inflation, currency exchange rates, interest rates, economic activity of the sector to which the new product belongs, and other. Macroeconomic issues, such as the impact of trade agreements and of the economic unification of Western Europe should be included. The effect, positive or negative, of current and anticipated government regulations should be assessed. Finally, the impact of social changes should be considered.
- Distribution: channels and need for support. The marketing research should identify the preferred distribution channel, the nature of intermediate marketers, and the extent of technical service needed to support the new product.

When marketing research is carried out in-house, a few guidelines must be kept in mind. Assumptions must be clearly stated, and conclusions derived based on a well-defined scenario (or alternative scenarios). Projections from the past should be avoided, but historical data should be analyzed so that projections can be interpreted in the light of what happened in the past. Projections must consider the markets underlying the demand for the new product. For instance, military needs and commercial aviation underlies the demand for airplanes; these systems underlie the demand for guidance systems, which contribute to the demand of certain electronic devices, and so on.

If data are obtained through interviews, careful preparation is of paramount importance. Interviewees must be selected carefully, and questions framed according to the position and personality of the interviewee. Finally, answers to the same question should be obtained from different sources constituting various viewpoints.

## Examples

Two examples are given to explain the potential of, and some of the problems affecting, marketing research. *Semiconductors* exemplifies one of the most detailed and reliable sources of marketing data. *Indium* shows the result of segmented analysis of historical data on the U.S. demand for this specialty metal and how historical data can be used as a base for projections.

### Semiconductors

The transistor is one of the most spectacular new products ever invented. This product and its derivative products not only revolutionized electronics: they revolutionized society. The transistor is a solid state device that permits signal amplification and switching. Its invention in 1948 opened an era characterized by many innovations that can be grouped into three categories: the perfectioning of discrete devices suitable for wiring into circuit boards; the development of integrated circuits where many devices (currently as many as 20 million) can be integrally constructed in a circuit not larger than one square centimeter; and the development of optoelectronic circuits, whereby electronic and optical signals collaborate in fulfilling a variety of functions. From the business viewpoint, discrete solid state devices, integrated circuits, and hybrid circuits are collectively called semiconductors (from the principal physical characteristic of the basic materials that make them functional), and the manufacturers are usually referred to as the semiconductor industry.

The transistor derived from the results of fundamental research, carried out at the prestigious Bell Laboratories. The original basic research was deliberate, in search of a revolutionary method for improving telecommunications. Not so in many other cases, where inventions either derived from acute observations of accidental events, or from an accumulated storage of basic information.

Computers existed before the transistor was invented. They depended on vacuum tubes. In the early fifties, a computer that today could fit in a hand calculator might have contained ten thousand vacuum tubes, used large amounts of energy, needed a thermostatically controlled room, and had to be operated by a significant number of specialists and maintenance personnel. Reliability was limited. Expansion of its capability would have further decreased reliability to the point of no return. The transistor, and later the integrated circuit, allowed to drastically decrease the size of computers and other electronic engineered systems, increasing their reliabilities and drastically decreasing their functional costs.

The semiconductor industry is blessed with an excellent marketing data base which is updated frequently and made available at moderate cost. For instance, the Electronic Industry Association and the Semiconductor Industry Association publish extensive marketing data periodically.

The Integrated Circuit Engineering Corporation publishes a more specialized and detailed report[8] on the integrated circuit industry. Segmentation is effected at different levels and with respect to different factors. This being an international industry, there is segmentation by region. This being a complex industry, there is distinction between captive and merchant markets. Technically, subdivision extends to types of products as well as functions. End uses are taken into consideration and much information is reported about the manufacturers, including their market shares.

How can a product developer make treasure of this wealth of information? It all depends on where the developer stands. If the goal is to develop a superior integrated circuit of given technical and functional characteristics, the references quoted and other information are valuable to frame such product in the context of the state-of-the-art. They may indicate past trends of demand for such products and their potential competitive products. They may give a reasonable picture of who is in the business, what fraction of the market is captive, and how foreign producers fare in their attempts to invade domestic markets. They may say much less about specific application areas, about values to users, and about anticipated rate of penetration in the market and growth. For all this, there is no substitute to specific and systematic inquiry in the field, but the perusal of this wealth of marketing information constitutes an excellent preparation for field marketing research.

### Indium

Indium is a low melting metal which has many industrial applications. In Figure 5.1, indium demand in the United States is given for 1973 to 1987, as reported by the U.S. Bureau of Mines.[9] The data show five end uses: metal products, instruments, electronics, nuclear, and others. These data are given as an example of what can be derived and cannot be derived from historical market data.

First of all, nothing can be derived unless the five end uses are defined. Obviously, this is impossible for the "other" category. At time this conglomerate of many minor applications becomes a substantial fraction of the total demand; unless it is segmented, the loss of information is significant. This is especially critical when the "other" category is growing, as in the case exemplified. It may contain a "dark horse" which should be recognized.

The substantial decline in demand for metallurgical products, instruments, and electronics in the early seventies may be significant and worthy of analysis. In the case of electronics, the analysis is simple: indium was used to "dope" germanium in the semiconductor industry, but when silicon was progressively substituted for germanium, it was no longer needed. Why, then, did demand not tend to zero in the long run? Mainly because, more recently, devices based on indium phosphide or similar compound semiconductors were developed.

An attempt to analyze in a similar manner the instrument and metallurgical products end uses runs into semantic issues. One finds that the instrument category may contain elements of other end uses. As for the nuclear end use, an analysis will uncover that the demand is a function of the underlying market (which is in decline) as well as of competition with other materials. These two elements must be sorted out.

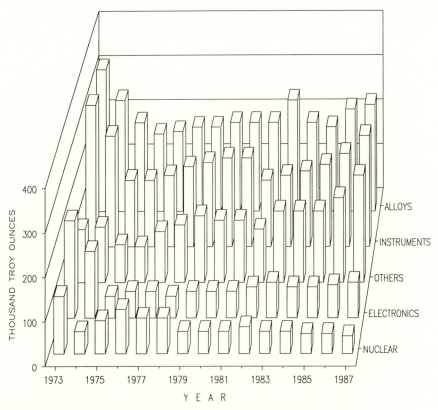

Figure 5.1  Indium Demand Segmented by End Uses, United States, 1973–87

*Source*: United States, Bureau of Mines, *Minerals Yearbook, Volume 1*. Various issues.

## Conclusions

In the beginning of the new product development process, a qualitative definition of market needs is sufficient and advisable. Later on, quantitative data are needed.

Marketing research is the mechanism by which quantitative market data are obtained. Its timing is very critical. It should be carried out repeatedly, first in a broad, albeit cursory manner; later in a more focused, but confined manner. Reiterations are essential.

Marketing research should include not only past and projected demand data, but also information on competition (both interproduct and interproducers), distribution channels, and external factors that are likely to affect demand.

There are many, relatively inexpensive sources, of marketing data. Even the best must be scrutinized critically with respect to the semantics of the information reported, and the primary sources of such information. Useful as they are, these readily acquirable data bases are seldom sufficient. Specific marketing research must be carried out.

Such endeavor can be implemented in-house or farmed-out. Most often, a combination of the two modes is preferred.

Projections should never depend on extrapolation of past trends. They should consider the underlying markets, application engineering issues, values to users, as well as many other factors including restructuring of the industry, government regulations, and societal changes.

Marketing research decreases the business risk of new product development and is useful to guide both technical and commercial development.

## Notes

1. I. S. Servi and R. I. Jaffee. "Metals Requirements of the Electric Power Industry." *Materials and Society*, 10, no. 3 (1986): 330.

2. United States, Executive Office of the President, Office of Management and Budget, *Standard Industrial Classification Manual* (Washington, DC: U.S. Government Printing Office, 1987).

3. United States, Department of Commerce, International Trade Administration, *1989 U.S. Industrial Outlook. Prospects for over 350 Industries* (Washington, DC: U.S. Government Printing Office, 1989). Published yearly.

4. United States, Department of Commerce, Bureau of the Census, *Current Industrial Reports*, various issues. Published periodically.

5. United States, Department of Commerce, Bureau of the Census, *1982 Census of Manufactures*, Compiled by: Berman Associates, Lanham, Maryland (Washington, DC: U.S. Government Printing Office, 1983).

6. Deborah M. Burek, Karin E. Koek, and Annette Novallo, *Encyclopedia of Associations 1990* (Detroit, Michigan: Gale Research Inc., 1989).

7. Dun's Marketing Services, Inc., *Dun's Consultant Directory® 1989* (Parsippany, New Jersey: Dun's Marketing Services, Inc., 1988).

8. Integrated Circuit Engineering Corporation, *Status 1989. A Report on the Integrated Circuit Industry* (Scottsdale, Arizona: Integrated Circuit Engineering Corporation, 1989). Published yearly.

9. United States, Department of the Interior, Bureau of Mines, *Minerals Yearbook, Volume I* (Washington, DC: U.S. Government Printing Office, 1973 to 1988).

# 6

# Analysis of New Product Ideas

## Introduction

Decision makers in business need to make choices among various alternatives. They must select personnel, distributors, sites for new plants, sources of new capital. Some choices are readily made, others are difficult and even critical; they may determine successes and failures.

Sound choices depend on an appropriate analysis of the alternatives, according to a disciplined methodology or according to subjective judgment and common sense. Irrespective of the analysis mode, each choice must be given certain attributes, else the procedure becomes a hit and miss.

In the new product development process, a business is confronted with alternative ideas and the resources available are such that only one, or, at best, a few can be pursued at any one time. It is therefore imperative to develop a method for analyzing these ideas, rank them, and select among them those that are worthy of pursuit.

Countless methodologies have been proposed to analyze *products*—that is, what has already been developed and, in certain cases, commercialized. In these cases, choices can be made after having acquired substantial knowledge of markets, producibility, and other critical factors. As an example Glasser[1] developed and recommended a product evaluation technique based on engineering, financial, marketing, and manufacturing considerations. He subdivided these areas into elements and explained how to proceed with the evaluation exercise. Elaborate methodologies of this kind, sound as they are, are seldom applicable for selecting new product ideas *before* committing sizable resources to their development, because insufficient information is available at that time.

In this chapter, a simplified methodology, not inconsistent with the more sophisticated techniques recommended by others, is suggested. This methodology will be exemplified, based on the assumption that a business enterprise is confronted with the need to make choices among a number of new product ideas in a static fashion; that is, at one point in time. In fact, new product development is a dynamic process. Its dynamic nature is handled by effecting subsequent reiterations of the static analysis as the new product development process evolves.

The portfolio of ideas should be kept evergreen by periodically replenishing it as it becomes depleted by the implementation of projects. Old ideas should not be discarded, because the dynamic and subjective nature of new product development may lead to their rebirth. There is, however, the risk that the quality of the portfolio will eventually deteriorate. In this case, creative sessions should be enacted to upgrade the portfolio quality.

The analysis of new product ideas invariably consists of three principal steps:

- development of ranking criteria,
- implementation and management of the ranking process, and
- selection of ideas for action.

Quite often the development of ranking criteria is given inadequate attention. Criteria should fit well the size, nature, and other characteristics of the enterprise and should derive from the consensus of several sectors of the enterprise.

The implementation and management of the ranking process is a somewhat easier task, once the ranking criteria have been soundly established.

Selection is, of course, the most critical step, and seldom derives only from the mechanical exercise carried out in the ranking phase. After all, the destiny planner (usually the general manager, often with the blessing of the board of directors) is ultimately responsible for final choices.

Ranking is often affected by constraints. Does the company have adequate resources? Does the product have market appeal? Are any regulations violated?

Constraints are of two kinds: hard and soft. The first kind comprises those that make an endeavor absolutely impossible. A perpetual motion machine cannot be developed. Other products that violate known scientific principles face hard constraints. A small business does not have the resources to develop a novel nuclear reactor. Certain weapons are banned by international law. These are other hard constraints.

Most constraints are, however, soft; that is, they can be removed by changing the environment, discovering a new technical approach, or developing new marketing channels. Caution should be exercised in ranking ideas without considering ways of removing soft constraints; but the removal of such constraints by trivial or unsound approaches is a delusion.

How is the analysis of new product ideas undertaken? An example will set the stage for answering this question. A manufacturing concern is currently selling prefabricated residences of modest price and limited surface area (say, 1,000 to 1,500 square feet), principally aiming at suburban customers. This company has, at a point in time, a portfolio of three new product ideas: a scaled-up (say, 2,000 square feet) and upgraded version of its current product, also catering to suburbia, but targeted to wealthier owners; a prefabricated utility shed suitable for present customers; and a prefabricated field office for construction companies. The scaled-up house is an example of a modified product for a new market. The prefabricated utility shed is an example of a new product for the current market. The prefabricated field office is an example of a new product for a new market. If the company has resources for implementing only one idea, how can it make a sound decision? How would it develop and apply ranking criteria? Who will make the final decision? These and other questions will be answered in this chapter.

## Development of Quantitative Ranking Criteria

The development of sound criteria to rank ideas quantitatively is very critical. There are two issues: *what* types of criteria best serve the enterprise, and *how* and *by whom* the criteria are developed. The *what* issue will further be subdivided based on

- relation to business strategies,
- soundness of scientific foundations,
- market needs,
- prior art, and
- company capabilities.

Some management science experts add another criterion by asking the question *is there a champion?* The importance of a champion—someone who deeply believes in the worthiness of the new product and is willing to take personal risk to support it—is great, even essential, in certain circumstances, but could be inconsequential in others, and, sometimes, even negative. Thus, we prefer to ignore this criterion.

### Relation to Business Strategies

The *why* issue of new product development is here reemerging. New product ideas can be ranked based on two criteria: company strength and business attractiveness (see Chapter 1). For instance, in the example concerning the manufacturer of prefabricated residences, from the technical and manufacturing viewpoints, all three ideas are in the area of company strength; from the marketing viewpoint, the utility shed is the most consistent with company strength, and the field office the least consistent. As far as business attractiveness is concerned, a cursory analysis may reveal that the upgraded and scaled-up residences rank highest, in view of the increased value of suburban land and of the improved affluence of suburban owners. The utility shed may rank lowest, because its unit price is modest, and severe competition is likely to limit the profit margins.

Most cases are much more complex. An analysis of business strategies may lead to the definition of ten or more ranking criteria, including the following:

- size of the investment opportunity;
- consistency with strategies of diversification;
- desire for backward or forward integration;
- plans to invade foreign markets;
- dependence on, or independence of, military projects;
- minimization of product liability risks;
- enhancement of company's image and stature; and
- synergistic effects with current products.

The list of criteria is very specific to each enterprise, to its size, stability, and overall character.

What if business strategies are ill defined? Forcing the definition of ranking criteria is often very helpful in recognizing the limitation of enunciated strategies. At times, it may induce the planner to take a step backward, review and revise policies and strategies, and then return to the definition of ranking criteria.

### Soundness of Scientific Foundations

Large, technically sophisticated companies have the means to assure that new product ideas have sound scientific foundations, because their technical departments are strong and because they have active systems of checks and balances. Occasionally, however, ideas are developed at substantial expense before recognizing fundamental scientific weaknesses. This may occur when development teams do not comprise members of all pertinent disciplines. A different type of unsoundness derives from ideas based on complex problem-solving approaches, when a much simpler route is viable. In these cases, soundness should be interpreted as consistency with the scientific basis that leads to the most efficient problem solution.

The problem with soundness of scientific foundations is most severe in small companies that attempt to invade new areas. Small companies are, generally, very knowledgeable in their own area of expertise and often exceedingly creative. Their internal flexibility permits generation and implementation of new product ideas not probable in larger and more complex environments. Occasionally small enterprises apply their creativity in areas of ignorance. They reap many initial successes only to realize later that insurmountable blocks are on the road.

Caution should be exercised in distinguishing between soundness of scientific foundations and soundness of engineering approaches. According to current scientific knowledge, heat will never flow naturally from a colder to a warmer part of an object. In any system that does not involve nuclear reactions, the energy input cannot be different from the energy output. On earth, a free object has essentially 100 percent probability of falling toward the ground. Violations of these scientific principles are unsound foundations of new product ideas.

Violation of scientific principles should be distinguished from the application of improper engineering practices. There is no guarantee, for instance, that a system that works in the laboratory will work if scaled up 1,000 times, but this is theoretically possible. The assumption that a new product idea is sound because a scaled-down prototype can be produced and work properly may be erroneous, but may not violate scientific foundations.

Another example is offered by a historical case. In the 1950s, a major chemical concern attempted to produce diamonds by applying an electrical field from a carbon source to a diamond seed. The experiment was unsuccessful; no growth was ever measured in the seed. At that time, some critics regarded such a simple scheme impossible, based on violation of scientific principles. In effect, the failure of this experiment might have been caused either by the application of an improper engineering practice, or by an unreasonable expectation of the rate of growth. Today, commercial production of diamond films by plasma chemical vapor deposition is a well established art.

Criteria based on scientific soundness of new product ideas can be developed by systematically analyzing the basic disciplines and theories on which the product stands.

## Market Needs

The issue of market needs was discussed at length in previous chapters. Needs should be expressed in both qualitative and quantitative terms. At times, qualitative descriptions are adequate to develop ranking criteria; but, more often, marketing research must be carried out before undertaking such endeavor.

Problems arise here, because marketing research on all ideas that are in a portfolio is prohibitively expensive. A compromise must be reached. Initially one may attempt to simply determine the order of magnitude of current markets, the past and anticipated future growth trends, the principal application areas, and other criteria that indicate the extent of market appeal and potential.

Other criteria may include the barriers to entry, the extent of competition, the need for technical services, the most desirable distribution channels, the price sensitivity, the value of reliability, the importance of aesthetic appeal, the influence of transportation costs, and the effects of government regulations.

Special attention should be given to whether the new product ideas fulfill an existing market need or create new needs. The second case most often ranks much higher than the first.

### Prior Art

In order to successfully develop new products, the knowledge of what in the market already fulfills *the same function* is imperative. This is how prior art should be interpreted. The knowledge of current products that compete directly is necessary, but it is not sufficient.

Criteria should be developed that indicate to what extent the new product idea may eventually constitute an improvement over prior art. They should also appraise the extent of proprietary protection of prior art and the probability of overcoming this barrier to commercialization. Proprietary protection of prior art is usually a soft constraint; it can be circumvented by licensing or joint venturing at the expense of part of the profitability. Yet, it must be assessed as early as possible.

Having identified as thoroughly as possible the prior art, the ranking criteria should be able to assess the degree of differentiation between the new product and prior art. Of course "me too" products are often viable; but differentiated products usually rank higher if they fulfill the market needs at least as adequately as current products.

### Company Capabilities

This set of criteria concern the exploitation of company strengths. Three areas should be explored: capabilities for technical development, for commercial development, and for manufacturing. In addition, consideration should be given to the company's financial strength.

Could a metallurgical company effectively develop a new product that requires biotechnology for its technical development and manufacturing? Is a commodity producer in a position to market specialty products, if the corporate culture is inconsistent with the new product line? Can a manufacturer of consumer products suddenly break into the military market with new products consisting of complex engineered systems?

Whereas joint venturing, acquisitions, and farmed-out services can extend the capabilities of a company, they are of no avail if the enterprise does not have its own strong foundations.

### Sources of Ranking Criteria

Having set the stage for the development of criteria, and identified the major areas to which detailed criteria belong, the question is how to generate a sound list. This is perhaps the most difficult issue to attack.

One approach is to identify a diversified group of persons, mostly internal personnel with some outsiders; some technical experts and others more commercially oriented; some conservative people and others very aggressive. Given certain guidelines and constraints, each person could be asked to generate a list of ranking criteria. This set of lists should be integrated (preferably by a person who did not participate in the generation of the criteria), duplications deleted, and items rearranged in a logical fashion.

Contributions by outsiders are very important. Often, members of the board of directors are eminently suited to participate in this exercise. Consultants are other sources of outside inputs. At times even major customers or suppliers may participate.

Time and resources permitting, the integrated and organized list of ranking criteria should be reviewed by all participants, and revised accordingly. Some participants are likely to change their minds in this second pass; the net result is a stronger framework to work on.

## Mechanics of New Product Idea Ranking

Given a set of ideas and a set of criteria, judgment must be expressed in quantitative terms, so that ranking can eventually be effected and the best ideas selected for implementation. One approach is to attribute to each criterion a *figure of merit* and a *weighing factor.* The first determines the *absolute* importance of that specific factor, without regard to other factors; the second the *relative* importance of that factor when compared with others. For instance, each factor can be given a figure of merit based on a ten-point scale, and a weighing factor ranging from zero to one. By multiplying each figure of merit by each weighing factor, and by adding all results for each idea, an overall rating number is obtained.

The next step is to rank the ideas, each of which now has a rating number attached. Unless the list of ideas has not been continuously revised and upgraded, one is likely to find that the rated ideas naturally divide themselves into three groups: a small group having very high rating, another small group having very low rating, and an intermediate section the elements of which are difficult to discriminate from their neighbors. Often a gap occurs between the high and the intermediate, and between the intermediate and the low group.

Should this three-way segmentation not occur naturally, two cutoff ratings can be established, or, alternatively, the groups can be formed by segregating the top 10 percent and the bottom 10 percent of all ideas.

Hopefully, this exercise generates a top group of ideas that requires, for its full development, more resources than are available. Otherwise, it is advisable to return to the idea generation process and to attempt to improve the quality of the idea portfolio. In this case, the ranking exercise will have been found very salutary in directing idea generation along promising paths.

The management of the ranking process is best reserved to a person or organization (whether internal or external) that is the least involved with the actual new product development process. The selection of such person or organization is most critical, and should take into consideration not only pertinent competence, but also the personalities of all participants.

## Examples

The principle and practices described above are reinforced by reciting two examples. *Quarry* is a hypothetical case of a mining company that wants to expand its product portfolio. It has found that its options are many, but the choice among them is difficult. This company asks a consulting firm to design and manage a product idea analysis process.

*Corfam* is an abbreviated history of a technically successful, but commercially unsuccessful, product; a synthetic leather developed by the Du Pont Company for shoe manufacturing.

### Quarry

Quarry, Inc. is a fictitious mining company that sells commodity industrial minerals such as limestone and potash. Its sales volume is on the order of 450 million dollars a year, profit margins are moderate; profitability has been reasonably stable. Its technical strengths are primarily centered around two focal points: superior knowledge in the evaluation of new mining properties and large scale engineering know-how. Technical know-how for postmining operations is more limited. Comminution and sizing are handled well, but additional processing is seldom needed in current operations. The company has excellent infrastructures and understands transportation economics very well.

From the marketing viewpoint, the company has an excellent understanding of current markets and is sensitive to both positive and negative events that may affect future business. For example, it has been following, with much trepidation, the decline of the big steel industry, a major outlet for one of its products. It has actively searched for alternative markets. It has realized that future stability must depend on diversification.

Quarry, Inc. is managed by a relatively conservative team. The board of directors ruled out diversification in new areas, such as metal mining, coal, and other product lines that would require realignments of both engineering and marketing activities. It wanted to capitalize on mining know-how, but understood that future opportunities will mainly depend on specialty minerals. Some of these specialty minerals can be upgraded, through postmining processing, to value-added products. The company thinks that it can eventually gain the appropriate technical know-how, as long as it has an opportunity to generate early cash flow from operations with which it is currently very familiar. However, it regards it safer to search for an acquisition target.

The company's planning group undertakes a cursory market search and identifies the extender-filler-coater product line as a potential area of opportunity. This area comprises a number of minerals, such as kaolin and mica, that are used by a variety of industries. These minerals might decrease the costs of plastics, rubber, or paper because they are less expensive than the base materials (extenders); they might improve the properties of the base materials (functional fillers), or they might create special surfaces on such materials (coaters). A more detailed, quantitative market research could possibly be carried out in-house, but thorough planning also implies specific, in-depth knowledge of mineralogy, process engineering, application engineering, industry structure, and the like. Quarry, Inc., therefore, decides to seek the help of a consulting firm.

After extensive interviews with several Quarry executives, representing general management as well as sector management and staff groups, the consulting firm develops this methodology. First it identifies five minerals that seem to fit the client's need. For each, it determines principal producers, total market, average price, principal application areas, and anticipated growth trends. Then, collaboratively with the client, it establishes the ranking criteria including the following:

- Financial

  Size of investment opportunity
  Business risk

- Technical

  Consistency with company know-how
  Need for substantial R&D

- Marketing

  Yearly revenue
  Growth trend

A rating scale (one to ten) and a weighing factor (zero to one) is then established for each criterion as indicated in Table 6.1. The rating exercise yields the results displayed in Table 6.2.

In this case, preliminary ranking is straightforward. Product C comes up on top, product E on bottom, products A, B, and D are close to one another and of intermediate rating. There is a gap between top and intermediate, and between intermediate and bottom. If there were resources for only one new product, the choice would appear simple: it will be product C. However, *exclusive* reliance on the ranking mechanics may lead to problems. The results of the ranking exercise must be scrutinized. Perhaps additional information is needed before reaching a final conclusion.

## Table 6.1.
## Examples of Project Rating Criteria

| CRITERION | LEVEL | RATING |
|---|---|---|
| INVESTMENT SIZE (m$) | 1 TO 10 | 3 |
| | 11 TO 70 | 8 |
| | 71 TO 150 | 5 |
| | 151 TO 200 | 2 |
| | OVER 200 | 0 |
| BUSINESS RISK | LOW | 10 |
| | MEDIUM | 5 |
| | HIGH | 1 |
| COMPANY KNOW–HOW | ADEQUATE | 8 |
| | NEEDS MAJOR UPGRADING | 6 |
| | NEEDS ONE NEW TECHNOLOGY | 4 |
| | NEEDS TWO NEW TECHNOLOGIES | 2 |
| R&D REQUIRED (% OF SALES) | UP TO 1 | 9 |
| | 1 TO 1.5 | 7 |
| | 1.5 TO 2 | 4 |
| | OVER 2 | 3 |
| REVENUES (m$/YR.) | UP TO 10 | 4 |
| | 11 TO 100 | 8 |
| | 101 TO 200 | 9 |
| | OVER 200 | 10 |
| GROWTH TREND (%/YR.) | UP TO 1 | 1 |
| | 1.1 TO 2 | 4 |
| | 2.1 TO 3 | 6 |
| | 3.1 TO 4 | 8 |
| | OVER 4 | 10 |

The exercise tells us the most appealing choice consists of a medium risk investment opportunity in the 10 to 70 million dollars range. This is well within the company's capabilities and consistent with corporate culture. But, are the revenues adequate to make a significant impact on a company that sells 450 million dollars per year of minerals? Certainly. The rating shows that the revenues are between 100 and 200 million dollars per year. A suspicion arises here: could such revenue really be generated with such a modest investment? If this were true, then this would be an attractive business in which the financial price of entry is low. Is competition likely to increase significantly in the future, squeezing profits out of the operation? Moreover, is the exceptionally

### Table 6.2.
### Rating of Five Products Based on Criteria from Table 6.1

| CRITERION | WEIGHING FACTOR | PRODUCT | | | | |
|---|---|---|---|---|---|---|
| | | A | B | C | D | E |
| INVESTMENT SIZE | 1.0 | 2 | 5 | 8 | 0 | 3 |
| BUSINESS RISK | 0.8 | 5 | 5 | 5 | 10 | 1 |
| COMPANY KNOW–HOW | 0.5 | 4 | 8 | 2 | 6 | 4 |
| R&D REQUIRED | 0.2 | 4 | 4 | 7 | 3 | 4 |
| REVENUES | 0.7 | 8 | 4 | 8 | 10 | 3 |
| GROWTH TREND | 0.9 | 6 | 4 | 10 | 1 | 8 |
| OVERALL RATING | | 19.8 | 20.2 | 29.0 | 19.5 | 15.9 |
| PRODUCT RANKING | | 3 | 2 | 1 | 4 | 5 |

high growth trend based on in-depth market research or is it only an educated guess? Is the low consistency with current technical know-how a risk factor not adequately represented in the overall rating? These and other questions suggest further, specific inquiries on the nature of product C.

Should resources be adequate for, say, two products rather than only one, the intermediate group needs to be analyzed further to be able to discriminate between its three members.

Product E, the Cinderella in this group, deserves additional analysis, to ascertain whether certain negative factors can be removed. Part of the low rating derives from the small current revenue; however, growth trend is substantial. Does Quarry, Inc. need immediate rewards, or is it stable enough to wait for long-term opportunities? The business risk is high. Could it be decreased through joint venturing? These and other factors should be considered before concluding that product E is not worthy of pursuit.

### Corfam

Not all products are successful. For instance, the Ford Motor Company met severe market resistance when it introduced its Edsel model, whereas it received enthusiastic responses when it introduced the Mustang. The purpose of this example is not to analyze the cause of a failure, but to speculate on

whether failure could have been foreseen. Could development costs have been saved when the product was only an idea? Incidentally, the successful Mustang, originally, was just a gleam in an executive's eye. He believed in the market appeal of a "poor man's Corvette"—an original, albeit qualitative, new product idea.

It is the case of a new product searching for a market. Du Pont's prestigious technical center developed, in the early forties, a synthetic moisture-vapor permeable sheet material. This material was considered to be a leather substitute, because leather is permeable to vapors. Further product and engineering process development, carried out at substantial costs, led to commercial production some 25 years after the initial invention. Subsequent marketing strategy was based on introducing this new material in relatively expensive shoes. Accordingly, the new material was priced high relative to leather (even though below initial cost).

In the beginning, market reaction was favorable; the product was continuously improved, as market feedback, especially with regard to finishes, was received. Problems arose later on. Because Corfam is elastic, it does not stretch permanently and conform to the feet as leather does; hence comfort was found wanting. Retailers recognized that the new material was introducing an added dimension to their inventory problems. Not only did they have to stock different shoe styles, finishes, and sizes. Now they needed to stock two distinctly different materials. The retailers became reluctant to advertise this new product line in a way that would give recognition to Du Pont's invention.

Another problem derived from a change in fashion, whereby vinyl-coated fabrics became popular as an upper material for ladies' shoes. Ironically enough, the introduction of Corfam by a prestigious firm gave respectability to coated fabrics.

For a variety of reasons, including foreign competition, adequate market expansion did not occur and the new synthetic material was eventually withdrawn from the market.

Giragosian[2] drew important additional observations from this history, among these:

- The immediate market for the new material was more limited than the original market research had indicated.
- The targeted market (fashion shoes) is highly unpredictable. What has appeal today may have no demand tomorrow.
- Catering to the unpredictable fashion is not consistent with the substantial technical and financial investment needed to produce the new material and improve its market appeal.

Could a more critical evaluation of the original new product idea have avoided losses? Could a different new product development orientation, based on identification of market needs followed by product development (rather

than searching for markets for a product already developed) have been more rewarding? Could a more creative analysis of market needs and a deeper understanding of the unpredictable nature of the fashion shoes market have put a limit to the investment-to-revenue ratio and to the development expenses needed to bring the venture to fruition? Could a more complete analysis of leather, the then current competitive material, have indicated that being vapor-permeable is not the only feature that makes leather appealing to shoe manufacturers?

We need not answer these questions to make the point that an in-depth analysis of new product ideas pays its dividends handsomely.

## Conclusions

To make choices is a way of life in business. Choices can be readily made when a large amount of precise and reliable information is available, but this is seldom the case. Moreover, the dynamic nature of business requires continuous information updating.

The critical importance of choices among alternate new product ideas is that they are made before substantial resources are committed to technical and commercial development. At this early stage of the new product development process, however, the foundations on which choices are made are, of necessity, fragmentary. It is, therefore, essential to follow a disciplined methodology and to cross-examine the results of new product idea analysis in a variety of ways.

The desirability of maintaining and continuously upgrading a portfolio of new product ideas has been emphasized in this chapter. Such a portfolio should contain more viable ideas than could be exploited with the means at hand. In this case, the first step is to develop ranking criteria.

To rank ideas, rating criteria must be identified based on company business strategies, market needs, prior art, company's capabilities, scientific soundness, and other factors. Such criteria, and their relative importance (weighing factors), must be developed by consensus, with maximum participation of the various company sectors. Contributions by outsiders, be they directors or consultants, are highly desirable.

Once a methodology has been developed and agreed upon, it must be managed, preferably by a reasonably detached member of the company team, or by an outside advisor. Given a large number of ideas in the portfolio, this ranking is likely to generate three groups of ideas; those rated high, those rated low, and those, often of similar value, rated in the middle. A gap often occurs naturally between the top and the middle, and between the middle and the bottom group.

At this point the results of the ranking exercise should be critically reviewed. Before selecting one or more of the top-rated ideas, each idea should be further scrutinized based on other considerations, some of which may be qualitative and subjective. Before discarding other ideas, the major constraints on which their mediocre ratings are based should be identified and consideration given to ways of removing such constraints.

Analysis of new product ideas, theoretically, should be founded on objectivity. But objectivity without creativity may lead to missed opportunities. Intuition often plays a very constructive role. Both excessive dependence on mechanical ranking methods and excessive reliance of subjective judgment lead to mediocre ultimate results.

## Notes

1. Alan Glasser, *Research and Development Management* (Englewood Cliffs, New Jersey: Prentice-Hall, Inc., 1982): 38–48.

2. Newman H. Giragosian, "Selected Case Histories of Commercial Development Projects—Case History: E. I. Du Pont de Nemours & Co.—Corfam." In *Successful Product and Business Development,* edited by Newman H. Giragosian (New York, New York: Marcel Dekker, 1978): 264–274.

## PART III

# HOW?—IMPLEMENTATION MODE

what we shall call the *implementation modes*. The choices of implementation mode are similar whether technical development is the responsibility of a one-hundred-member, well-funded, interdisciplinary team or by a lonely inventor.

Implementation, whether technical, commercial, or financial, consists of three principal elements and issues:

- The definition of essential activities,
- the identification of resources needed to implement a plan, and
- the solution of problems.

## Implementation Modes

In this discussion implementation modes will be described in a generic fashion, without consideration for whether they pertain to technical, commercial, or other forms of development. Essentially, there are five different modes of implementation:

- in-house
- farmed-out
- licensing
- joint venture
- acquisition

These modes are *not* mutually exclusive. Often a judicious combination of two or more modes is most effective. For the sake of clarity the discussion of these five modes will be described as if it were the sole basis of implementation.

The *in-house* mode implies that all the actions are carried out within the confines of a given business enterprise. In the case of a single-plant operation that sells directly from the home office, this mode can easily be visualized. Two or three sector managers have adequate staff to completely implement the new product development process. Everything is carried out under one roof. Communications are streamlined. Coordination and critical decisions by the general manager are prompt. There is little probability of misunderstanding. Timing is readily optimized. Problems may, however, arise from lack of critical skills or resources.

At the other extreme, for a multinational, multidivisional corporation, *in-house* implementation can acquire a variety of modes. Are all developments implemented within a single profit center? Is technical development centralized or decentralized? In how many locations will the activities be carried out? How are the various activities coordinated? From the vantage point of a minor foreign subsidiary, in-house activities implemented by, say, a central research

# 7

# Implementation of New Product Development

## Introduction

The hypothetical company (described in the preceding chapter) seeking new products has now completed its new product development planning. It has defined its corporate objectives and strategies, evaluated the current product portfolio in terms of company strength and business attractiveness. It has identified qualitative market needs, quantified essential facets of such needs, stimulated the creation of more new product ideas than the company could possibly implement, evaluated and ranked those ideas, selected one or more ideas for action, and critically reviewed the selected ideas for consistency with company strategies.

The company has exhaustively answered the *Why* and *What* questions and is staged for action. Now it must answer the question *How*.

The implementation of new product development is specific for each company and business environment. Only broad generalizations are feasible. The most appropriate mode of operation must be selected after appraising a company's capabilities, identifying the major strengths and weaknesses, and reviewing periodically such appraisal and identification as internal and/or external events may warrant.

This chapter emphasizes what can be generalized and what is reasonably applicable to all aspects of the implementation process. This chapter introduces the next two chapters, which will describe two principal action areas technical development and commercial development.

The intimate interrelationship of technical and commercial development a fundamental principle of successful new product development. All too often technical and commercial developments are separated by differences in human skills, organizational structure, imperfect communication, cultural differences, and timing. These differences and the conflicts they generate can be accommodated, once they are recognized.

Another common weakness is the lack of imagination in the design and selection of the alternative ways in which developments can be implemented laboratory appear farmed-out. At times, conflict of interests are likely to arise. The successful development of a new product may benefit greatly one strategic business unit while causing hardship to another. Collaboration and cooperation is unlikely to occur naturally; they must be fostered. Line organizations may not be able to function properly without an overlay of staff functions. The destiny planners are not always readily available for critical decision making.

Complete farming-out of new product development is seldom feasible and hardly advisable. It is, however, possible. For example, an inventor has conceived a new product idea based on a software package that can improve the effectiveness of certain high school teaching. The inventor can depend on a consulting firm for marketing research, hire a free-lance software specialist for the technical development, review the resulting product, ask a patent attorney to apply for patent protection, hire a consulting firm for test marketing, and negotiate a contract with a distributor. Even when experimental research and development is necessary, the same general sequence of activities may be effective.

As the difficulty of the task at hand increases, due to the number of technical skills needed for proper implementation and to the complexity of the marketing operation, it is unwise and often impracticable to farm out completely the entire process. A hybrid mode (in-house and farmed-out) is much more effective.

The major problem arising from the farmed-out mode is the lack of direct control on operations that determine the success or failure of the venture.

Licensing generally means the acquisition of proprietary rights for the manufacture and marketing of a product. It may carry limitations with regard to geographical areas, end use, and other operational factors. The meaning of licensing is here extended to signify permission to manufacture and/or distribute a product that is new to the company acquiring such permission. Therefore it includes permission to sell, but not to manufacture, in which case the licensee, even if capable of manufacturing, acts only as a distributor. It includes franchises, that is, the exclusive right to market a product or service in a limited area, contingent upon meeting certain minimum performance standards. It also includes the permission to manufacture any product based on a proprietary process. These products may be new to the market or only to the licensee. If manufacturing is involved, a certain amount of in-house technical development may be necessary.

Licenses often carry the licensor's obligation to offer technical services, product advertising, or other means to assist the licensee. Licenses imply the payment of royalties, and therefore decrease the profit margins when compared with the exploitation of products for which the seller has proprietary rights. Exceptions occur, especially in the case of products developed at taxpayers' cost, as those derived from government projects. Exceptions may also occur in the case of products developed by a company for the benefit of its customers. As an example, the producer of a commodity raw material may embark in application engineering R&D and develop, say, new grades of steel that need such raw material. The commodity producer is likely to give its customers royalty-free licenses. This is contingent on the assurance that the customer is capable of manufacturing quality products and undertakes appropriate marketing effort.

The meaning of joint venture is also subject to various interpretations. It could mean a joint technical effort aimed at developing a new product by combining the skills of two or more companies, with certain agreements about distribution rights and partition of pay off. For instance, a pharmaceutical company and an instrument manufacturer may decide to embark in a joint venture R&D project aimed at the development of a control release pump for the delivery of a new, powerful drug. The pharmaceutical company brings to the party its knowledge of the potential, limitations, and hazards of the new drug; it also brings its know-how concerning relations with physicians and health care organizations. The instrument company brings to the party engineering know-how and manufacturing methods. Both parties benefit from the successful completion of the joint venture. Each adds a new product to its portfolio. Either could operate independently from the other, gaining operational flexibility, but decreasing the probability of success.

Joint ventures may concern products that have been already developed. As an example, the manufacturer of a home appliance has developed a new product, but has ascertained that domestic manufacturing is excessively costly. It negotiates a joint venture with a foreign company well known for its productivity in manufacturing. It may also negotiate, at the same time, a licensing agreement for the distribution of the new product outside the domestic area.

The last mode of implementation implies acquisition of an operating company. Generally, an acquisition entails an expansion of the product portfolio of the acquiring company, even though no innovation is involved in this case because the products are already on the market and new only for the acquiring company. Acquisition usually entails a review of the combined portfolio, and the shedding of products, or product lines that do not fit in the strategic plans of the combined enterprise.

Acquisition may lead to the commercialization of truly new products, whenever the acquired company has experimental products that can be brought to market using the financial resources of the acquiring company.

## Principal Implementation Elements

In any implementation mode, a company must define essential activities, needed resources, problems and their solutions. These elements cannot be defined in generic terms. They depend on the type of development (technical or commercial), on the mode of implementation, and, especially in the case of problems, on contingent and immediate factors, relating to the specific product or to the environment.

A certain degree of generalization is, however, possible. For instance, activities must ultimately prove that the new product satisfies a market need. Activities must be legal, acceptable to society, physically implementable. They must not interfere unduly with current operation; they must be carried out with reasonable confidentiality so their outcome will not help the competition.

Needed resources always include human and financial resources. A physical plant, office, or other buildings must be available for development implementation. There must be an organization to monitor, coordinate, and control the endeavor. As a house cannot be built depending only on its blueprints, so a new product cannot be created depending only on ideas.

Problems are ever present. They exist at the onset of the implementation phase, and keep appearing later on. Problems are not destructive *if the problems of today are different than those of yesterday.*

Problems are inherently related to the dynamic nature of state-of-the-art advancement, just as stresses are inherently related to dynamic nature of life. In his book *Quantum Healing*,[1] Dr. Chopra compared life stresses to the energy of ocean waves: to the timid surfer, waves represent a threat and are a cause for anxiety but to the confident one they are the principal source of his enjoyment. So are problems. They do not exist only in situations that are static and unchangeable. They can be devastating to those who approach them with trepidation, but they can also be a principal stimulus for creativity and a source of satisfaction when solved.

New problems often appear after the new product has already reached the market. If not removed, the development process remains incomplete. They may concern the physical characteristics or the functional performance of a new product. They often derive from societal acceptance, eye appeal, or relation to other products that are not well positioned in the market. They may derive from conflict of interest within complex enterprises.

In all cases, *the solution of a problem begins with its accurate definition.*

## Examples

The *Pilkington* example generalizes the removal of a technical problem by an imaginative solution that depends on letting nature assist the inventor. It also indicates how a widespread licensing policy helped a major industry. *Cooling Tower* shows the degree of flexibility that often exists in the selection of modes of implementation.

### Pilkington

Window glass used to be manufactured by rolling hot glass. The resulting product was far from smooth and its optical quality was, therefore, marginal. To improve surface and optical quality, flat glass had to be painstakingly ground—a time-consuming and expensive operation. The market needed an improved and inexpensive flat glass, but such a goal was regarded as unattainable if only based on modifications of the basic manufacturing method.

In 1952 a glass manufacturer, the Pilkington company, conceived the idea of floating molten glass onto a bath of molten tin. This approach solved a major technical problem by letting nature do a tough job. After removing the constraint caused by the rolling equipment, the glass naturally assumed a smooth surface because of its desire to minimize its internal energy. The glass became reasonably strong at a temperature that was still above the melting point of tin. By slowly cooling one end of the tin bath, the glass plate could be readily handled and removed.

Pilkington could have prevented its competitors from exploiting this proprietary invention. It decided instead to license it to all qualified manufacturers. The invention became a major innovation and diffused reasonably rapidly throughout the industry.[2] At least in the United States, virtually all flat glass is now manufactured by this float process.

### Cooling Tower

This is a hypothetical example, which is, however, partially derived from a historical event. A cooling tower is an engineering component used to remove unwanted heat from a fluid stream. It can often be found in utility and chemical plants.

The Acme Company invented, manufactured, and marketed a novel cooling tower consisting primarily of molded polymers rather than fabricated metals. Such product had several advantages over competitive products already marketed with regard to resistance to corrosive environments and durability, but was less energy efficient. Marketing was very successful until the oil embargo drastically increased the cost of energy. The position of this product on the market suddenly became unfavorable, compared to competitive units.

Acme believed that a decrease in energy consumption necessitated a complete redesign. Having decided to bring a new, energy-efficient, product to the market, it had three options: design it in-house, farm out design and prototype construction, or look for a current product that could be licensed or otherwise acquired.

Farming-out was ruled out, because in-house capabilities were at least as good as those that could be found elsewhere. Licensing appeared a much better proposition. A search among domestic manufacturers failed to identify a product meeting the technical specifications wanted. The search was therefore extended to foreign countries. Finally one such product was uncovered, made by the Nadir Company, in a less developed country of limited political stability.

Before discussing licensing agreements, Acme investigated Nadir, and found that its product did not sell well, even though technical specifications were very appealing. Soon Acme discovered that the poor market acceptance was because Nadir's cooling tower consisted of many parts that had to be joined together by the customer; this was a labor-intensive operation and a possible cause of limited long-term reliability. Licensing, therefore, appeared to be a risky proposition.

Acme considered a joint venture, but discarded that idea, because it realized that transfer of engineering know-how to a company operating in a politically unstable country was not in its best interest. It considered acquiring Nadir, but decided not to adopt this mode because too many of Nadir's other products were of no interest to Acme.

All five modes of implementation appeared undesirable. An impasse? Not necessarily—only a problem to be solved. What Acme needed was to combine the energy efficiency of Nadir's design with the ease of installation and reliability of Acme's design. Acme's engineers searched for the elements of Nadir's design that imparted high energy efficiency. They identified a limited number of components and realized that these components could be readily incorporated in Acme's unit.

Another round of negotiations was then started between the two companies. After exploring various options, the two companies agreed that Nadir would become a long-term supplier of specialized components to Acme. Nadir would receive from Acme an adequate compensation for these components, It would also become an exclusive distributor of Acme's cooling towers in a limited geographical area.

## Conclusions

The implementation phase of new product development should be undertaken with the same open-mindedness, creativity, and flexibility as the planning phase.

There are five principal implementation modes: in-house, farmed-out, licensing, joint venture, and acquisition. Each could, by itself, be viable, but more often a combination of two or more modes lead to the most rewarding results.

Technical and commercial developments should always be carried out in unison, and maximum integration should be fostered between these two principal aspects of new product development.

Consideration should be given to the dynamic nature of the new product development process. The mode of implementation, as in the case of planning, must be periodically reviewed and, if appropriate, revised.

Implementation is made up of three elements: activities, resources, and problems. Activities must be legal, acceptable to society, consistent with capabilities, and related to objectives. Resources include human, financial, and physical. Problems are ever present and should constitute challenges rather than causes for anxiety or dismay. They are the spark that stimulates creativity. Their solution always begins with valid definitions.

## Notes

1. Deepack Chopra, *Quantum Healing* (New York, New York: Bantam Books, 1989).

2. Fay V. Tooley, Ed. *The Handbook of Glass Manufacture*, 3rd Edition (New York, New York: Ashlee Publishing Co., Inc., Books for the Glass Industry Division, 1984): 714–718.

# 8

---

# Technical Development

## Introduction

Technical development is defined as the set of activities that is needed to reduce a new product idea to practice. Technical development always begins with a concept that evolves progressively and becomes a concrete entity. Its evolution continues until the embryonic entity becomes a viable article of commerce or service. Technical development is akin to animal gestation.

The outcome of gestation can be an abortion, a marginally vital offspring that needs careful nurturing, a permanently impaired, but otherwise viable, offspring, or one that is in all respects healthy and anxious to grow. Immediately after birth, the offspring is not capable of independent operation. It must be cared for, fed, and sheltered until weaning is advisable. A time may come when excessive sheltering is harmful, rather than useful. This is the time to let the offspring fight in the world based on its own capabilities.

In this chapter, the essential activities, the resources needed, and the main problems affecting technical development will be highlighted. Human resources, organization, communication, and management support will be discussed in subsequent chapters.

Technical development may range from a solo operation—the traditional garage inventor mode—to the multidisciplinary, complex team spanning across many organizational units, sometimes involving more than one corporation. The concepts enunciated in this chapter essentially apply to all modes of operation, but the major emphasis will be placed on technical development implemented in a well-directed industrial laboratory of sufficient size to permit the interaction of various specialists. The direction of technical development should be akin to the direction of a symphony orchestra, rather than to the driving of an oxen team. The skilled conductor directs, but does not drive. He pulls out the skills of the individual players, but does not push. He inspires, coaches, and gives a unique tone to the collective effort.

In addition to direction, administrative and technical support are needed in order to optimize the output of the skilled individual members of the team. The destiny planner must keep reminding all the players and coaches of the ultimate goal, lest the enthusiastic drive of the inventors carry them along unrewarding paths.

In the management science literature, technical development is segmented into research and development; research may be subdivided into fundamental, basic, oriented basic, and applied. These classifications have limited significance because they depend on the research mode rather than on the research objective. Unfortunately, they are often used as a foundation for establishing the organizational structure.

Focus on objective is a better and more functional way of classifying technical development. In his classic book *The Management of Industrial Research*,[1] E. Duer Reeves recommends to classify technical development according to whether activities aim at:

• defining future business objectives or
• fulfilling well-defined business objectives.

Reeves calls the first group of activities *fundamental and exploratory research* and suggests keeping the specific new products or processes ill defined, focusing instead on the principal goal—to define businesses that are consistent with company strategies and capabilities. Reeves recommends earmarking a fraction of the available resources to fundamental and exploratory research—perhaps 10 to 15 percent of the total—and to keep that level constant irrespective of company fortunes.

The previously mentioned case of the development of the transistor at Bell Telephone Laboratories is a classic example of fundamental research. When that research was first launched its objectives were defined as follows:[2] "The research carried out under this case has as its purpose the obtaining of new knowledge that can be used in the development of completely new and improved components and apparatus elements of communication systems." Specific new products or processes were not defined, nor was a specific business goal enunciated such as, for instance, to diversify into the manufacture of devices for chemical process control. The only business emphasis consisted of reiterating that the company offered telecommunication services and, therefore, was seeking improved apparatus elements.

Numerous examples of exploratory research can be found in the development of chemical or pharmaceutical compounds. In these areas, product mortality is very high, and success often derives from accidental happenings coupled with keen observations of potential applications, or from semi-empirical testing of a large number of new products. The specific definition of a business objective during exploratory research is not only unnecessary, it unduly limits the long-range opportunities that may derive from the technical development.

The fundamental and exploratory research, when carried out at a consistent level of effort, has the additional function of preserving certain critical skills whenever there is no need to implement major technical projects.

Reeves calls *project R&D* the technical activities aimed at fulfilling a well-defined business goal. The level of resources must be commensurate to the task at hand and to the magnitude of payoff. Essential skills can usually be identified in the planning stage. Direction must be firm and relentless. Project R&D may concern complex engineered systems such as a supersonic plane, a space capsule, or a telecommunication network as well as simpler consumer products, but in all cases a definitive market need consistent with company's strategic objectives and capabilities must be identified.

Technical development is also useful to enhance the company image, but the creation of a separate classification of activities to fulfill this function is unnecessary. Quality exploratory and project R&D yields by-products that are more than adequate to improve company image. The justification of technical development activities because of their publicity value only is unwise.

## Essential Activities

This section concerns only project R&D, as previously defined. We assume that the business objective has been clearly stated. All activities aim at fulfilling that objective.

A number of activities are essential for the development of any product. Their nature may vary according to the type of product being developed. A software package and a nuclear reactor, for instance, need product design, but the implementation of this activity is very different in these two cases. For the sake of clarity essential activities will be described for a single type of product—a relatively simple engineered system, such as an analytical instrument, a consumer appliance, or an automatic weapon.

### Product Definition

Before embarking into technical development, the product to be developed must be defined as well as possible, especially with regard to the functions that must be fulfilled to satisfy a market need. (A review of Chapter 3 will prove beneficial.) For example, a more expedient way of collecting tolls in highways and bridges constitutes a well-established market need. (We are neglecting the fact that technical development in this area is well under way.) A product fulfilling this need may be defined as an engineered system that senses the passage of a vehicle, identifies the vehicle in a unique fashion, and records the event. In its simplest form, this system produces a written record of the events, after sorting them out according to some predetermined criterion, such as license plate number. In its more sophisticated form, the system computes the toll and charges a credit card or other account that matches the vehicle identification. The system must have a very low level of error. It must generate a signal, or record an image of the vehicle, whenever a vehicle that is not creditworthy intersects the sensing element. It may also be programmed to flag those vehicles that are wanted for other reasons.

At this stage of new product development, the specific nature of the product need not be defined, but consideration should be given to other factors, such as the influence of weather, the vulnerability to intentional foiling, the maximum speed at which it must be operational, and the sensitivity to dirt accumulated on the vehicle.

### State-of-the-Art Survey

The project team must then ascertain whether such a new product concept has ever been reduced to practice, and, if so, whether it is already an article of commerce. This state-of-the-art survey is carried out by undertaking a search of the open literature, a patent search, and a review of commercial engineered systems that even remotely may be of value, such as supermarket or airline baggage optical scanning systems. Finally, the project team must keep its ear to the ground at technical meetings, trade shows, and elsewhere, and gather intelligence on competitor's activities.

The information gathered is then analyzed by comparing what was learned with the functional product definition. Should a proprietary system or useful component be found, whether commercial or not, the feasibility of an acquisition, licensing, or joint venture should be explored before embarking into technical development. The state-of-the-art survey is also useful in evaluating proprietary positions that may interfere with future manufacturing and marketing activities.

### Product Design and Engineering Feasibility

Given the functional objectives, the limitations created by competitors' activities, and the availability of useful components, the engineering team designs a system. Engineering design is likely to reveal that some 90 percent or more of the components are readily available, reliable, and within reasonable price ranges. The balance is not. Focus is then concentrated on the removal of these bottlenecks. Here is where creativity and know-how comes into play. Bottleneck removal may be effected by developing a new critical component, or by eliminating its needs by changing the rest of the design.

The design finally appears reasonable, but feasibility is yet to be demonstrated. An experimental model is then constructed, often by first fabricating, testing, and improving individual components, and then by integrating these components into a working system.

The system is tested and, invariably, found deficient in certain respects. The analysis of the reasons for these deficiencies is a critical step in the new product development process. If correctly implemented this analysis will either establish a base for the removal of the deficiencies or conclude that the design is so faulty that a complete redesign is mandatory. In the first case further technical development usually leads to a successful demonstration of engineering feasibility. In the second case the project reaches a major decision point: abandon or return to the beginning of the design stage.

## Pilot Planting and Prototype Production

The functioning of an experimental model is no assurance of ultimate success. Concern is now focused on industrial producibility. According to the operations needed to manufacture the new product, and to the manufacturing capabilities of the company, the construction of a processing pilot plant may or may not be needed. Here, scale-up problems often occur. For certain products, such as an integrated circuit, scale-up signifies an increased throughput rather than a major increase in equipment size. In the extreme case of a commodity product, scale-up invariably signifies a change in equipment size, at times by a factor of one thousand or more. For example, the technical development of a new stainless steel suitable for a very corrosive environment can be implemented in the laboratory in batches of one hundred pounds, and in the prototype stage in batches of one ton. Economic production may imply processing equipment that handle batches of 100 to 200 tons. The pilot plant must be designed not only to prove the producibility of the product at the one-ton scale, but also to define the engineering parameters needed for the construction of the full-scale production plant.

Whether a pilot plant is needed or not, the experimental model must be manufactured under conditions that approach those of an industrial operation, and the product design may have to be somewhat modified to improve market appeal. Such modification often aims at improving ruggedness. The resulting product is not yet commercial. It is a prototype, suitable for internal and field (often called *alpha* and *beta*) testing.

## Field Testing and Industrial Producibility Demonstration

Throughout the previous activities, the technical team has worked in parallel with the commercial team. Initially, the commercial developers have supplied information on market needs, competitive activities, market potential, pricing, and the like. At an appropriate time, sites for field testing are identified. The prototype is offered to selected potential customers for testing. Feedback is critical and sometimes biased; technical developers must be intimately involved in field testing, but further action must be decided by consensus, or by a product manager accountable for the ultimate success of the development.

Simultaneously, consideration should be given to industrial producibility. Based on the nature of the product, processing scale-up may or may not be necessary. If it is, a major engineering effort may be in order. Industrial producibility issues include factors other than technical—typically, the skill of the available manufacturing workers and supervisors, environmental control, waste stream disposal, and safety.

### Product Adaptation

The product prototype seldom fulfills the market needs and seldom can be produced routinely without product adaptation. Such adaptation may consist of making minor changes in order to improve eye appeal, adding a missing feature, decreasing manufacturing costs, or substituting scarce raw materials. Even more substantial modifications may be consistent with the basic design concept.

Unfortunately in certain cases product adaptation is not feasible because it would require a complete redesign. The new product may have to be abandoned.

For the surviving new products, the adaptation phase is very important and often critical. The simile of the newborn animal still holds. The newborn is an engineered system potentially equipped to function in a variety of environments. To actualize its potential, it must become adapted to specific environments and life-styles. As the newborn grows, new capabilities are acquired. As it ages or as handicaps develop, it can make up these deficiencies by adaptation. If it does not adapt, it will sooner or later perish. In all cases, life will come eventually to an end. At that time, the perpetuation of the species will depend on replacement which, in our context, signifies the development of other new products. The product cycle is never-ending.

The importance of product adaptation is shown in the early days of certain highly innovative consumer products. These products have evolved with time. Could the outstanding growth of television have occurred, if the picture always consisted of the roundish, small, black and white, low-definition image of old? Do we remember the early sepia tone Polaroid pictures or the original Edison phonograph with its wax cylinders?

One may question whether the responsibilities of the technical development team ever end. Fundamentally they do not, as long as a product is alive. In practice, the development team must continue to monitor and assist each new product beyond the point of its transfer to routine production. The team should not hold on excessively to it, lest too few resources are left to rejuvenate continuously the product portfolio. A happy medium must be struck.

## Essential Resources

In-house implementation of technical development requires many resources, including:

- human
- financial

- facilities
- supporting services
- organization and management

Deficiencies in any one of these resources lead to substandard performance even when the other resources are outstanding. Countless examples could be quoted of superb facilities backed up by ample financial resources and staffed by very skilled manpower that were closed after a few years of operation because of inadequate organization and management. Examples also abound of imaginative and well-organized technical teams that, short of achieving success, were starved of supporting services and financial resources when confronted with contingent economic pressures.

The ranking of various types of resources is a futile exercise. As in the case of a symphony orchestra, no player can be truly called more important than the others. A superb concertmaster cannot make up for an out-of-tune oboe; the musicians who carry the main melody cannot compensate for the supporting portion of the orchestra.

Should one be forced to choose the most important factor affecting the ultimate outcome of technical development, undoubtedly human resources will come up on top—principally because a single, very imaginative and knowledgeable member of the team can often pierce through the most difficult blocks encountered en route and lead the entire team to success.

The dream of having a technical staff composed of individuals who have many skills in one skull is today hardly achievable. Science and engineering are far too complex. Interdisciplinary teams are usually essential. However, total dependence on specialists, even if coordination and direction are very effective, is hazardous. The presence of one or more broad-minded generalists is very desirable.

Even when most activities are implemented in-house, the dependence on outsiders is salutary. Contributors who are not permanent members of the technical staff may range from occasional consultants, needed primarily to supplement the regular staff in highly specialized areas of science and engineering, to part-timers and temporary employees. Students often inject into the operation a different approach to problem solving and an enthusiastic perception of what is doable. Unfortunately, administrative rules, such as a stiff interpretation of head count ceilings, sometimes prevent the utilization of highly desirable and often inexpensive human resources.

The technical team should be diversified not only with regard to principal skills, but also with regard to personal background and culture. In pre-World War II times, when in the United States most technical teams were fairly homogeneous culturally, the chief technical executive of a major industrial research laboratory made a practice to recruit in Europe, presenting, from time to time, a number of "different" employees to the somewhat dismayed laboratory director. This practice caused frictions in the daily operation. Answering the director's complaints, the executive stated that an effective laboratory should be like a quiet pond in which an occasional catfish has been tossed. Today, an excessively homogeneous staff is no longer a problem.

The assessment of financial resources needed to implement technical development is an arduous task because of the many uncertainties that confront technical operations. There is virtually no limit to what a technical organization can consume. Thus a rationale should be developed to determine what is essential, what is adequate, and what is optional. Because technical development is labor intensive, most companies limit financial resources by placing ceilings on manpower. The wisdom of this practice is questionable because, to a great extent, there is reasonable flexibility in the utilization of money. Services are readily acquirable, and some capital investment can lead to time and manpower savings. To limit somewhat human resources has, however, merit in one regard: the level of full-time technical staffing should, if at all feasible, be no higher than what is sustainable in the long run. Frequent expansions and contractions of technical staff undermine morale and may be very disruptive.

The establishment of a technical budget based on an arbitrary percentage of sales revenue is even less desirable than a limitation of manpower. Rather, financial resources should relate to the anticipated magnitude of payoff and to the risk that the operation entails.

Much has been written on facilities. Except for the value of facilities as a means to attract outstanding technical personnel, functionality should be the main criterion. Some operations require special facilities such as clean rooms, explosion-proof building, and so on. Except in these cases, facilities, and especially their cost, bear little relation to the effectiveness of technical development. Attention should, however, be given to the effect of facilities on communications between team members. A technical center tends to become informally compartmentalized, often because of the location of team members. Facilities that promote informal exchanges and induce people to mix to the maximum extent possible are beneficial to technical operations. The General Atomics laboratories in La Jolla, California is one of the best examples of facilities designed with this concept in mind. All general services are housed in a round building. Offices and laboratories are located in a concentric, annular construction, thereby making each location equidistant from the service building. At one time, staff was spatially randomized by seeing that adjacent offices and laboratories were occupied by personnel belonging to different organizational units.

The selection of the location of technical development facilities is often critical. In the case of a single business unit, single plant company, all facilities are best located in a single site. A detached technical center is likely to be less efficient, even though it is preferred by those companies that are seeking major diversifications. In the case of multidivisional, multiplant companies, the site location becomes more difficult. Much depends on the degree of organizational centralization that one wants to achieve. The only possible generic recommendation is to guard against excessive isolation and excessive interference by day-to-day operational problems. Excessive isolation leads to partial detachment from business objectives, and is seldom compensated by periodic meetings. Excessive interference can be avoided by establishing separate facilities for separate technical functions.

The selection of equipment is even more critical. The obsolescence of scientific equipment is rather rapid and its cost high. The choices between alternative techniques, let alone vendors, is very wide. Who should make selections—the technical specialist, the middle manager, or the laboratory director? These selections are often unorderly and time consuming and can cause morale problems.

In case of doubt, supporting services should be made available generously to the prime technical developers. Most important among these are the information services. What used to be called "the library" is no longer adequate. An effective information center equipped with modern retrieval systems and staffed by skilled and cooperative personnel is one of the prime needs of technical operations. The optimum degree of centralization of technical support depends on the nature of the individual organization. Two problems are likely to arise in this regard. One originates from services that are too lean or of marginal quality. In this case, the prime technical staff is saddled with routine drudgeries that undermine overall efficiency. The other problem originates from services that are excessively possessive, thereby preventing the technical staff from gaining access to specialized equipment and personally experimenting with such equipment when, in their opinion, this mode of operation is beneficial.

Technical development needs organization, management, and control. These resources will be described later (see Chapter 11) when the *Who* of new product development will be discussed.

## Main Problems and Their Solutions

Problems are the spice of life. If recognized early and accurately defined, they can be attacked effectively and usually solved, making the organization stronger and more mature. Problems may derive from faulty technical development operations (mainly caused by deficiencies in the above-mentioned essential resources), but the most severe problems have different origins. In this regard, by far the major problems derive from faulty business planning or from the imperfect enunciation of business goals.

Two common complaints often verbalized by technical developers are: *they* do not know where they want to go and *they* do not tell us where they want to go. Why *they* rather than *we*? These complaints indicate lack of defined business goals and lack of identification with such goals. They may also indicate another problem that shall be discussed in details in Chapter 12, namely inadequate communication. All business persons plan, but not all communicate their plans to those who ought to know them, and few communicate their plans in terms that are understandable to the listener. An increase in return on investment by a given percent means a lot to the general manager preparing for a presentation to the board, but, what does it mean to the electronic engineer who is designing a high definition television system?

Problems arise when technical developers have inadequate knowledge of the market and of the competition. In the first case the cure is, as repeatedly recommended, to undertake technical and commercial development in parallel rather than in sequence. In the second case collaboration with the marketing department is valuable and outstanding information services are useful, but not sufficient. The technical staff must be sensitive to the war games of the business world. This sensitivity is seldom innate in individual members of the technical staff, but can and should be developed. Sensitivity to competition must be fostered continuously, as a part of personnel training.

The technical developer is likely to become emotionally involved with the task at hand, and the more difficult the task the deeper is such involvement. This is, per se, healthy, but often leads to a problem: excessive preoccupation with the technical elegance and sophistication of the new products rather than with their functionality. The search for simplicity should be, but seldom is, in the mind of the developer. Simplicity often means reliability and low cost. Ultimate performance is seldom critical; lack of reliability can be devastating.

Another common problem is to address industrial producibility only after substantial resources have been expended in technical development. To what extent industrial producibility can be assessed in the early stages of new product development depends on individual products. What is always possible is to keep industrial producibility in mind, looking primarily for those insurmountable blocks that may relegate an outstanding invention to the role of a laboratory curiosity, never to see the light of day.

Should a technical center be directed to avoid internal competition? Not necessarily. Certain centers have deliberately put two teams at work, one to prove that a new product is valuable, another to uncover what is wrong with it. Others have approached the fulfillment of a single business objective by establishing two technical teams, each following a different method of attack. Internal competition is often very stimulating and ultimately effective. Excessive internal competition may, however, be disruptive. The technical director is the principal arbiter. One catfish in the pond is healthy, but too many may lead to disaster.

Perhaps the major problems in the implementation of technical development concerns the entire organization rather than each individual project. The lack of long-term rejuvenation of the technical capability is the principal problem, often not recognized until its cure becomes very difficult or expensive and time consuming. A capability is more than a staff, a physical plant, equipment, financial resources, and supporting services. A capability can be disrupted and at times destroyed by a major project failure, leading to the need to curtail the staff, as well as by a major success, whereby a well-knit team is disbanded and partially transferred to a profit center. In the latter case, one may be winning a battle just to lose the war.

## Alternative Modes of Implementation

The preceding sections principally referred to technical development implemented entirely in-house. In effect, at least a part of the technical activities is always farmed out. In certain cases, entire projects are joint ventured or contracted. As an example, a company seeking major diversification in an area in which it has limited technical strength may ask a contracting organization to establish a facility, hiring a staff, and managing a project. This contract may contain the option of absorbing facilities and staff, contingent upon the results of the project.

Certain minor divisions of large corporations may select to farm out new product development to technical centers of other divisions or to a corporate laboratory.

All such schemes are, at times, most expedient and crowned by success, but caution should be exercised about ultimate accountabilities. The best persons to rear children are not necessary their fathers or mothers; but fathers or mothers should always feel accountable and monitor all the happenings.

## Examples

Two examples are offered. *Purity* shows the various implementation options that a successful corporation of limited means has when it decides to expand its product line. *Sun* describes the path followed by a technical team, related problems, and their solutions.

### Purity

Purity is a fictitious corporation that manufactures non-residential water purification systems based on a sophisticated technology such as electrodialysis. Total sales have reached 35 million dollars per years and are headed for sustained growth. The company has established a firm position in the market but is concerned about the limitations of its product portfolio. Diversification appears in order.

All of the company's activities are carried out at a single site, including technical development that is implemented by an aggressive team of twelve people. The team principally includes physical chemists and chemical and mechanical engineers. Supporting services are modest but adequate, considering the limited product line.

The general manager asks a consulting firm to undertake a diversification study. The consultant carries out this study in close collaboration with the director of planning and the technical director and recommends that one of these potential product lines be considered for implementation:

- Residential water purification systems, based on technologies with which the company is very familiar.
- Microanalytical instruments similar to those that the company and its customers are using to assess the effectiveness of the purification systems.
- Industrial systems capable of purifying specialty chemicals and pharmaceuticals, based on both familiar and unfamiliar technologies.

The first choice appears attractive, because it can be implemented after minimal technical development. The company recognizes, however, that marketing tactics are likely to be very different from those practiced so far. Moreover, success in this product line will undermine the market for the bottled water which originates from major current customers.

The second choice has appeal in terms of overall growth potential because of the ever-increasing occupational safety and environmental control regulations, but it depends on technical skills that are not ample within the company. The company, however, has been an extensive user of these products. It knows the competition well, and can assess value in use.

The third choice requires substantial application engineering and technical service; moreover, know-how is not easily transferable when serving customers that produce different chemicals.

The management team concludes that the microanalytical instruments have the greatest long-term potential, and decides to adopt this choice. But how can the technical development be implemented?

A review of competitors' activities indicates that most instrument companies allocate 10 to 15 percent of sales to technical development, whereas Purity typically allocates 4 percent. The adequacy of financial resources is in question. A review of available technical skill reveals the necessity of major staffing. The facilities would be somewhat strained, but otherwise adequate. A modest expansion of current buildings could generate all the needed space. Organization and management need not be altered.

This review leads to the conclusion that the project is viable but risky. Because the potential payoff is very large, joint venturing could be considered. The general manager, therefore, seeks a partner who has already a reasonable technical capability, and negotiates an agreement based on which most technical development will be done by the partner, and product alpha testing by Purity.

This example indicates that flexibility in the mode of implementation permits the realizations of dreams that are otherwise unattainable.

## Sun

This example describes a set of actual events. Shortly after the oil embargo of 1973, solar energy appeared to be an outstanding area for new product development. Kennecott, then an independent corporation and the largest domestic supplier of commodity copper, visualized the opportunity of developing copper-base solar absorber plates—the heat exchangers that absorb energy from the sun and transfer it to a fluid medium. At that time, there were two major lines of solar absorber plates, a very inexpensive line depending on plastic materials and a much more durable line based on aluminum. Because at that time aluminum was substantially less expensive than copper on a weight basis and even more on a volume basis, the necessity of using thin stock became obvious.

It just happened that one of Kennecott's subsidiaries, Chase Brass and Copper Company, was a major producer of thin copper strip, used by the automotive industry for making radiators. This mass-produced commodity appeared to be priced right, but would it do the job? Would it offer too much resistance to heat flow because of its limited thickness?

Technical development was implemented at the corporate center. The team responsible for developing several copper-base new products had outstanding material engineering skills, but limited mechanical or chemical engineering capabilities. These needed skills were, however, available in other organizations and projects of the corporate technical center.

The team acquired the part-time services of a mechanical engineer, who was mainly assigned to a high priority project. Although the engineer could devote limited time to the development of the copper solar absorber plate, design problems were quickly solved and a broad base patent protection obtained. Meanwhile, the experimental team proved that the thermal efficiency of a plate based on that design was at least as good as that of competitive aluminum-base plates.

A pilot production line was rapidly set up and plates manufactured in sufficient quantities to undertake a well-instrumented field test which confirmed all expectations. Armed with these data, the pilot line was expanded and experimental sales undertaken. The pilot line revealed industrial producibility problems that were overcome by minor design modifications.

The history of the commercial development effort and its outcome will be described in the next chapter.

This example principally indicates how the technical success of a project often depends on specific product definition and on the selection of critical skills. It also shows how much can be accomplished with limited resources when adequate attention is given to planning and direction.

## Conclusions

Technical development activities are best classified according to whether they are implemented to *define* or to *fulfill* business objectives. The first type of activities—basic, fundamental, and exploratory—should be funded at a preset level of effort and maintained irrespective of pressures generated by high priority projects or economic stresses. These activities are also valuable in maintaining a permanent core of the technical establishment and for training purposes.

Implementation of technical development aimed at fulfilling business objectives requires the most precise product definition possible, thorough state-of-the-art surveys, skillful product design, preliminary engineering feasibility demonstrations, and, in due course, prototype production and pilot planting. Market research and commercial development must proceed with excellent coordination and collaboration simultaneously rather than sequentially.

The essential resources needed to implement technical development besides finances are human resources, adequate facilities and equipment, supporting services, and an organization that can direct, manage, inspire, and control.

Problems invariably arise in the course of technical development. Problems commonly originate from faulty business planning or inadequate communication of business goals, excessive preoccupation with the elegance and technical sophistication of the new products at the expense of functionality, inadequate attention to industrial producibility at an early stage of the development process, excessive internal competition, and depletion of the technical teams caused either by personnel reductions in times of economic stresses, or by transfers when major successes are achieved.

All such problems are preventable or curable when direction is effective and when the technical staff receive continuous and appropriate training.

### Notes

1. E. Duer Reeves, *The Managment of Industrial Research* (New York, New York: Reinhold Publishing Corporation, 1967).

2. Bell Telephone Laboratories, *Authorization for Work—Solid State Physics—The Fundamental Investigation of Conductors, Semiconductors, Insulators, Piezoelectric and Magnetic Materials*, July 1945.

# 9

# Commercial Development

## Introduction

The long-term viability and growth of new products require continuing commercial development. Very few products create their markets in an effortless way because of their outstanding price/performance features. In such rare cases the competition closes in rapidly because the business potential is obvious to all.

New product development rests on three legs: business planning, technology, and commercial development. The third leg, commercial development, cannot sustain all burdens by itself even when business objectives have been defined well and technical development has been successfully completed.

New product development is dynamic: everything changes at all times. Success depends on reiterations of all essential activities.

Commercial development consists of defining specific market targets for a new product, assuring that its performance and price are consistent with market needs, promoting its existence and proving its worthiness, establishing marketing policies, strategies, and tactics, defending against competitive activities, identifying technical and other improvements that increase market appeal, determining the price elasticity in the short and in the long term—that is, how much the market volume is likely to decrease (or increase) when the price decreases (or increases), abiding with government regulations, responding to societal reactions, establishing distribution channels, and much more.

Literature and organizations concerning commercial development abound. Examples thereof will be quoted, but should not be regarded as a comprehensive catalog of what may assist the new product developer. Literature on commercial development often refers to a narrow product line such as specific consumer products. While very valuable, the information contained therein may not be readily transferable or adaptable to other product lines such as industrial materials.

In this discussion of commercial development, essential activities, resources, typical problems, and their solutions will be highlighted. In addition, marketing strategies and tactics will be described.

# Essential Activities

## Competitive Analysis

Commercial development has limited effectiveness unless it is preceded by competitive analysis. Such analysis should start by determining the structure of the organizations that produce and/or market similar or competitive types of products. The determination of industrial and commercial structures is today difficult in view of frequent mergers, acquisitions, divestitures, and joint ventures. Most information is in the public domain; some is not, and requires skillful intelligence. Difficulties are usually more severe when foreign competitors are involved, a very frequent occurrence.

Industry structure must include distribution channels, their functioning, incentives, and limitations. For instance, about one-half of the stainless steel produced in the United States is distributed directly to the ultimate users from the factory. The rest reaches the ultimate users either through the service centers, principally distributors, or through reprocessors, that reroll, polish, coat, and otherwise modify the products received from the factory to suit individual users. Effective commercial development implies thorough knowledge of these external distribution channels.

Competitive analysis must include a thorough definition of the new product and a comparison with whatever may compete with it. Special attention should be paid to the identification of alternative products that are *functionally* competitive, even though very different in nature. As an example, pesticides bear no physical relation to cotton seeds, but insect-resistant cotton seeds, engineered by biotechnology, compete functionally with pesticides.

## Product Differentiation

Product differentiation is, most often, a very critical element of success or failure. Even in the case of fungible commodities, some product differentiation is usually feasible. If the product per se is hardly distinguishable from competitors' in terms of performance and price, at least it can be differentiated based on deliveries and customer services. Today, an effective marketing practice for differentiating fungible commodities is to offer the disposal of waste streams originated in customers' operations. For instance, the suppliers of lime needed for the operation of scrubbers of electric power plants may acquire a privileged marketing position if they offer their customer the service of taking back the gypsum produced during the scrubber operation.

## Customers and Market Analysis

Another essential activity preceding actual development is the customers analysis. This analysis goes beyond the identification of potential customers and their quantitative needs for the new product. It must include an understanding of the nature and culture of the customers' environment. Technical know-how, negotiating style, risk taking, financial strength, and ability to back integrate are but a few examples of the characteristics and attitudes of customers.

A reasonable understanding of the downstream marketing structure must be gained. The producer of aerospace titanium alloys may sell one of its product lines only to a limited number of forging shops. These, however, may sell their products to jet engine manufacturers, who sell to aerospace companies, who sell to either airlines, individuals, corporations, or the military. This multilevel customer structure and its behavioral patterns must be understood.

### Product Testing

Commercial development is ultimately responsible for appropriate product testing, both in-house (the so-called alpha testing) and in the field (beta testing). The technical team is intimately involved in these activities, but the commercial team has prime responsibilities. The selection of beta sites is an especially critical facet of these activities.

The necessary involvement of technical personnel in beta testing may cause difficulties, whenever such personnel does not permanently belong to the marketing organization and has not received adequate training. All new products have flaws and limitations. A skilled marketing person is likely to defuse negative reactions by customers in various ways, assuring that all problems can be solved in time. The untrained technical specialists, however, may enunciate derogatory remarks that become imprinted in the customer's mind. Such remarks are likely to emphasize the barriers to product improvement, and occasionally state that a problem cannot be solved. Effective team effort and training pay its dividends.

### Promotion

Having proven the new product in the field, commercial development continues with promotional activities, generally spreading from an initial market niche to other promising marketing areas. During this process, commercial development principally aims at effecting sales growth, but also gathers intelligence concerning the value of product adaptation and the market needs for other products. In short, commercial development also fulfills the function of marketing research.

The techniques for new product promotion vary according to the product nature. A first step consists in preparing advertising brochures. All too often these contain inadequate *performance* data even though they may describe *product properties*. The customers want to know how they can receive a benefit from switching from a proven product to one that does not have a track record. They want a seller who demonstrates these features to consider the customers' environments and needs.

In these brochures the reporting of extensive data, based on the expectation that the customers will select the few data that are significant to them, is usually ineffective. At times, the preparation of different brochures emphasizing the product performance from the viewpoint of different applications and customer needs is much more effective.

The eye appeal of these brochures has merit and, with modern printing methods, can be achieved at reasonable cost, but it must be backed up by facts and figures.

A new product can be launched using different media. Press parties are reserved for special situations. Presence at trade shows, though rather expensive, is very effective, so much more if paired with technical presentations at the same site. By far the most popular medium is advertising in buyers' guides, produced by publishing companies and often included in magazine subscriptions. When the market target can be reasonably well identified, calling directly to selected customers is the most effective medium. Whether to influence first the customer's engineering department or the buyer depends on the specific product and on the customer's purchasing policies.

The commercial developer of a new product should always assume that the customer is very busy. The customer must be enticed to listen, to read, to compare. The use of short videotapes, left with a potential customer during a brief personal call, is most effective in many cases. These tapes can be perused after hours, have major visual impact, and can deliver much information in a very short time.

Promotion is a double-edged sword. The enthusiastic commercial developer is likely to promise more than the product can deliver. This practice is undesirable, especially when the embellishment is excessive. Honesty is, after all, a virtue, even in commercial development!

### Customer Service

Finally, an effective customer service function must be established. For a new product, this function may constitute a very expensive proposition. Customer service may include installation, application engineering, trouble shooting, and often training. Most software packages could not be marketed unless the frustrated user has immediate access to tutorial assistance. Even though such assistance is often built into the package, the access to a person who can answer queries has an out-of-proportion psychological value.

Customer services must also include prompt intervention when the customer complains about a major problem. Whether such problem has been caused by the product, by incompetence in its use, or by extraneous factors is immaterial.

Commercial development cannot stop at this stage in the product life; it must continue, often at a reduced level of effort, into maturity. This transition may involve organizational issues, especially when the product is substantially new, but does not constitute the kernel of a new strategic business unit. The incorporation of a new product line into a business unit comprising only mature products may highlight organizational deficiencies.

## Resources

The company that intends to diversify by developing an entirely new product line having a substantial growth potential may opt for the creation of a mini-profit center comprising all essential functions, headed by a product manager who is *de facto* a general manager with full profit accountability. When the new product is a modification of an existing one, or an addition to a homogeneous and well-established product line, commercial development may be implemented by members of the marketing department. In all cases, resources primarily consist of manpower, supported by considerable funds for market analysis, product testing, free samples, promotion, travel, and other essential activities. A special physical facility is seldom needed.

Commercial development need not be implemented only in-house. At times, it could be farmed out completely to appropriate service organizations. More often the in-house principal effort is supplemented by the support of public relation agencies, specialized testing laboratories, lobbying groups, and legal assistance concerning proprietary protection, product liability, antitrust considerations, and other issues.

Certain products require major experimental application engineering effort. Usually these endeavors are carried out by technical departments, but in some circumstances the commercial development team may include special facilities and organizations for this purpose.

The optimum level of commercial development depends on the nature of the product and on contingent circumstances. As for technical development, there is virtually no limit to the funds that may be applied to commercial development. Competitive activities may serve only as an approximate guideline.

## Strategies and Tactics

Generalization of strategies and tactics is dangerous. A company's business strategies, financial strength, and positioning often dictate the most desirable choices. For this reason, one approach to commercial development is based on strategic marketing. According to J. F. Cady and R. D. Buzzell,[1] strategic marketing should "create and sustain competitive advantage" rather than merely obtain "satisfaction of customer at a profit." Competitive analysis, evaluation of company strength and long-term vision, and the projection of future business environment are consistent with the strategic marketing approach.

The essence of competitive analysis—an essential foundation of strategic marketing—and the most effective technique for implementing such analysis in an industrial environment have been described by M. E. Porter.[2]

R. McKenna[3] emphasized the importance of product, market, and company positioning. In this author's view, an important key element of *product* positioning is the product differentiation based on intangible attributes, such as reliability and services. *Market* positioning greatly depends on inference. For this reason, the selection of the first few customers is critical because of its impact on subsequent commercial development. Consistent with the concept of strategic marketing, McKenna stresses the importance of knowing where a company is heading, and recommends internal *and* external auditing to ascertain the *company* positioning. The importance of relying upon persons or organizations not intimately involved in day-to-day operation could not be emphasized enough. Members of the board of directors are often in an excellent position to carry out effective external auditing.

McKenna recommends another recipe for success: concentrate on creating new markets rather than capturing a part of competitors' market share.

An intriguing description of commercial development tactics is found in the videotape *The Military Metaphor* by Kotler.[4] The author describes five attack tactics and six defenses that are akin to tactics and defenses of war games. As an example of the bypass tactic, in the semiconductor industry the device density of memory integrated circuits continuously increased as new products were developed. Whereas in the United States the manufacturers placed nearly equal emphasis on all densities, in Japan emphasis was placed on those selected density levels which were expected to become most popular. This strategy paid off; Japan captured the market lion's share of some products that had much higher demand than others. The selection of the specific products on which to concentrate requires superior market intelligence.

Many examples of the preemptive defense tactic are found in new product development. This tactic depends on striking before the competitor does. There are, of course, risks. Being first often means giving the competitor the opportunity to learn from the pioneer's mistakes, to discover product weaknesses without impairing market positioning, and to bring improved products to market.

F. E. Webster, Jr.[5] specifically addressed commercial development of industrial goods and services. He described the special seller-buyer relations that characterize this class of products and discusses, among other issues, the function of the industrial distributors. These distributors fulfill a much more critical function than the wholesalers and retailers of consumer products.

Most strategies and tactics recognize the importance of acquiring a reasonable market share. This concept is sound when the market share is well defined. Definition must be based on *available* rather than *total* market. A fraction of the total market may not be available for selling to because it is captive or because it is inconsistent with a company's capabilities. Markets are always heterogeneous aggregates, even though they may appear homogeneous. For instance, for any one company, the available market for integrated circuits is never the total market of 10–15 billion dollars per year. A substantial fraction is captive. Moreover, many integrated circuit producers are capable of fabricating only certain types. Whereas a business plan goal may represent only 1 percent of the total integrated circuit market, it may be 20 percent when it is based only on the types of circuits that a company is able to produce, and 30 percent when captive markets are excluded.

Pricing constitutes one of the most critical aspects of commercial development tactics. For new products, the introductory price may be deliberately above or below cost. The first tactic, if successful, helps to recover development costs and may, at least in the case of certain consumer products, reinforce image of "new and improved."

An introductory price below cost recognizes the customers' contributions to field testing and future product improvements and may, therefore, be helpful in promoting initial sales, especially when the customer may be exposed to significant risks when using the product.

Pricing policies should take into consideration short-term and long-term price elasticity, that is, the increase (or decrease) in demand as the price decreases (or increases). Whenever prices are, in the long term, related to costs, a feedback mechanism operates because increased demand usually generates cost reduction due to economy of scale, which eventually leads to further demand growth.

Long-term price elasticity is somewhat predictable and may bear little relation to what a buyer is willing to pay for a product in the short term. Normally, sensitivity to price is higher in the longer than the shorter term.

Because in the long run prices are usually related to costs, the anticipated experience factor—that is, the decrease in product costs as a function of cumulative production—should be assessed. All products follow this pattern, but at different rates. For instance, the cost of crushed stones decreased by a factor two in forty years; the cost of integrated circuits by the same factor in four years. In both cases, cumulative production increased by a factor ten in the time period stated.

## Typical Problems and Their Solutions

Many problems arise during the fragile initial commercial development. Most can be anticipated and avoided. Some depend on the dynamic nature of the environment, and must be solved contingently by aggressive and prompt actions.

One of the most common problems is the overestimation of available market. The difference between available and total market has been explained before. One possible cause of such overestimation is excessive reliance on customers' expressed needs. Customers always have interest in stimulating competitions, and therefore in projecting future demand in an optimistic fashion. We do not suggest the prevalence of deliberate, dishonest practices. Optimism may be based on the customer's overestimation of his market, for instance. For this reason, market assessment should be based on different viewpoints and, if at all possible, should include independent opinions, as explained in Chapter 5.

Another common problem is the underestimation of competitive reactions. Consideration should be given not only to the reaction of direct competition, but also to functional competition between products. Some competitive products are of a different nature than the emerging new product. In the previously quoted example of insect-resistant cotton seeds, the developer of the improved seeds must assess what progress pesticide producers have made in creating products that are more acceptable ecologically and less prone to lose their efficacy with prolonged use.

A problem that may not be obvious in the initial phase of commercial development, but that may create major difficulties later on, is the poor understanding of the distribution channels. To what extent are they equipped to handle the new product? Do they have strong relations with manufacturers of competitive products?

Assuming an initial commercial success that exceeds expectations, new products may fail because of the inability to produce adequate supplies to satisfy the market. Such inability may be caused by financial constraints, by excessive lead time for expansion of manufacturing facilities, by inadequacy of distribution channels, or by problems requiring product and process modifications. Reliability of future supplies is a very important feature of new products. For this reason, sole sources are often at a disadvantage. Considerations should therefore be given to controlled development of alternative sources.

A new product that is well accepted and that can be delivered in adequate amounts may still be disappointing from the business viewpoint because of faulty pricing policies. This problem is very specific to individual products and competitive environments; thus a universal solution cannot be articulated.

Finally, a new product may be unsuccessful because of improper market, product, or company positioning (see McKenna). These problems are alleviated by appropriate new product planning. When insurmountable difficulties are encountered within the company, joint ventures should be sought.

## Examples

Of the numerous new products developed, only a small fraction achieve commercial success. Many others achieve technical success, but do not lead to tangible payoffs because of factors that may or may not be anticipated. The disastrous demise of asbestos products, for instance, is a prototype of a commercial failure based on findings that could not have been anticipated at the time these technically successful products were developed.

*Sun* is a sequel of the example given in the previous chapter, and describes a new product that had a short commercial life. *Thermo Electron* is an example of a success story based on strategic marketing.

## Sun

In the previous chapter, the successful technical development of a light, all-copper solar absorber plate was described. Before reciting the history of its commercial development, the structure of the developing company, Kennecott Corporation, is explained.

Kennecott was, at the time this product was developed, the largest domestic producer of commodity copper, with a throughput of some 400,000 tons per year. It had a subsidiary, Chase Brass and Copper Co. (CBC), a major fabricator of brass mill products, including the copper strip used for the manufacture of the solar plate.

The original objective of this technical development project was to increase the demand for both primary copper and for copper strip. These objectives were not, however, strongly founded, because the anticipated maximum additional market represented at best a very small increment over total sales of commodity copper, and because brass mills can use, if they so selected, 100 percent scrap, rather than virgin metal.

For CBC, incremental sales were more significant. Competition for copper strip was, however, very strong; thus this development was expected to help competitors as well. Assurance of this incremental sales depended on manufacturing the plates within the corporation, thus creating a captive market for CBC. However, neither the primary copper division of Kennecott nor CBC, being commodity producers, expressed interest in embarking on this business. Direct benefits could therefore be reaped only by creating a new profit center.

Technical development was implemented at Kennecott corporate technical center, and the ensuing patent was assigned to the parent corporation. The original technical development team prepared a business plan which was reviewed and endorsed by a prime management consulting firm. This plan established the cost effectiveness of thermal solar heating in residences of various regions of the country, demonstrating economic viability contingent on two principal factors: petroleum prices and government incentives.

The business plan overestimated projected petroleum prices and did not consider the fact that energy is pervasive, and therefore an anticipated increase in energy costs would be reflected, at least partially, on the manufacturing costs of the new product.

Notwithstanding the optimistic overestimation of petroleum costs, the analysis concluded that thermal solar heating would be economically attractive only for hot water, and not for space heating, unless government incentives prevailed.

The business plan for the creation of a new profit center was submitted to management and promptly rejected. However, the development team obtained permission to seek a buyer of this embryonic business, via an outright purchase of proprietary rights or licensing agreement. The buyer was found in Butler Manufacturing Company, which saw a merit in the project per se and also visualized a potential captive market since that corporation was the constructor of commercial buildings.

The new owner set up a subsidiary and built two manufacturing plants, one on the East and one on the West Coast. This operation was initially successful, but eventually declined, as energy costs decreased, and the government did not enact the incentives that were anticipated.

This example raises a significant question. Should a major commodity producer have sponsored a technical development that would at best have generated a product inconsistent with its marketing capabilities and business objectives? This question cannot be dismissed with the accusation of faulty business planning. Costs for technical and initial commercial development were modest, and were essentially recovered after the sales of proprietary rights. The development had publicity value, especially at a time when energy conservation was very popular. And, after all, energy shortage could have persisted long enough to allow this new product to become well established, in which case the experience factor could have made it economically viable, even in the light of subsequent decreases in energy costs.

### Thermo Electron

The history of Thermo Electron Corporation represents an example of successful strategic marketing.[6] During thirty years of operation, its founder and chief officer, Dr. George Hatsopoulos, planned new products by anticipating societal problems and carrying out the technical development in ample time to have the products on the market when demand materialized. Following this strategic marketing policy coupled with superior technical development capabilities, this company increased its sales revenues by a factor of ten from 1976 to 1988. Consistent with this strategy, during the 1982–1984 recession, profitability was deliberately impaired by increasing technical development activities, in order to be ready to reap benefits during the following boom cycle (see Figure 9.1).

Typical of this strategy was the emphasis on energy-conserving new products, implemented two years *before* the 1973 OPEC oil embargo. The need for such products was principally determined by comparing the energy consumption of the United States with that of other industrialized nations. Other anticipated needs included the decontamination of hazardous and radioactive

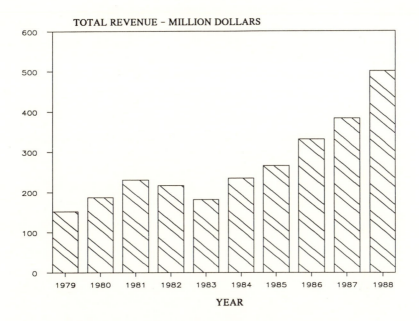

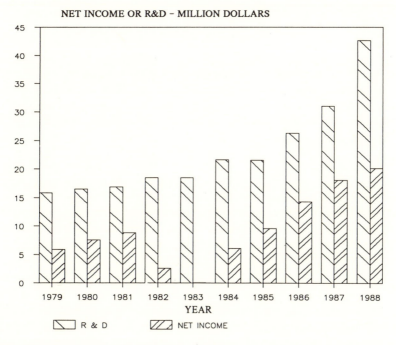

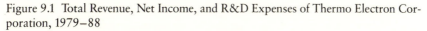

Figure 9.1 Total Revenue, Net Income, and R&D Expenses of Thermo Electron Corporation, 1979–88

*Source: 1988 Annual Report.* Thermo Electron Corporation.

waste, the detection of drugs and explosives, and, lately, the need to alleviate the so-called greenhouse effect.

## Conclusions

Commercial development is a comprehensive set of activities, including the establishment of strategies, the analysis of competition, the design of aggressive and defensive tactics, the proving of the new product with regard to market needs, the differentiation of products from competitors', the establishment of effective customer service activities, the formulation of a pricing policy, and the creation of distribution channels. These activities are likely to be partially implemented in-house and partially farmed-out.

The most effective commercial development is based on strategic marketing, whereby the activities create and sustain a corporate advantage rather than merely satisfying customers' needs in a profitable manner.

The principal problems are likely to stem from:

• overestimation of the available market;
• underestimation of competitors' reactions;
• lack of coordination between business planning, commercial development, and technical development.

Commercial development should concern not only the position of the new product in the market, but also the position of the company. Judicious selection of initial sales targets are critical in enhancing the company positioning, especially in the case of emerging enterprises or of radically new products.

## Notes

1. John F. Cady and Richard D. Buzzell, *Strategic Marketing* (Boston, Massachusetts: Little, Brown & Company, 1986).

2. Michael E. Porter, *Competitive Strategy—Techniques for Analyzing Industries and Competitors* (New York, New York: The Free Press, a Division of Macmillan Publishing Co., Inc., 1980).

3. Regis McKenna, *The Regis Touch. Million-dollar Advice from America's Top Marketing Consultant* (Reading, Massachusetts, Addison-Wesley Publishing Co., Inc., 1985).

4. Philip Kotler, Consulting Author, *The Military Metaphor*, 3/4″ U-matic Format Videotape, Part of a Series Entitled "The Great Marketing Wars," Produced by Burton Kaplan Company, Distributed by Prentice Hall, 1984.

5. Frederick E. Webster, Jr., *Industrial Marketing Strategies*, 2nd Edition (New York, New York: John Wiley & Sons, 1984).

6. "The Thinking Man's CEO," *Inc.*, 10, No. 11 (November 1988): 22–34.

# 10

# Protection of Intellectual Property

## Introduction

The United States Constitution states: "The Congress shall have power...to promote the progress of science and useful arts by securing for limited times to authors and inventors the exclusive right to their respective writings and disclosures."[1] Such writings, disclosures, and, in modern times, recording of sounds, video, and computer software are collectively called intellectual property. They are intangible assets, and therefore they have a value.

Statutes have been enacted to protect intellectual property.[2] This is a highly specialized field of jurisprudence; what is presented here should be regarded only as a cursory guide. It is offered primarily so that those involved in new product development can better relate to their legal advisors.

The larger corporations usually maintain an in-house staff for this purpose; others may depend on outside firms, in which case internal liaison personnel are often appointed to expedite the proceedings.

This chapter will describe the principal types of protection available in the United States, and will highlight the main problems that may arise.

## Types of Proprietary Protection

### Patents

Patents constitute limited monopolies which exclude others from making, using, or selling an invention. Patents are valid for up to 17 years from their date of issue. Why does a free market economy deliberately institute monopolies? Are patents inconsistent with legislation concerning restrain of trade?

This limited monopoly is granted in exchange for the publication of information that may otherwise be kept secret. This regulation stems from the philosophy that publication of trade secrets stimulates future inventions. The society as a whole benefits, whereas it would be hurt by an unlimited and unrestricted restrain of trade.

In the United States patents are granted to a person who invents any process, machine, or composition of matter which is new or improved *and* useful.

Patent protection has been extended, in recent years, from tangible articles and processes to software and to life science products.

In the patent law, *new* signifies whatever is not known or used by others, and not described in public documents. It also signifies what is not obvious and cannot be anticipated at the time the invention was made, by one of ordinary skill in the art to which the subject matter pertains.

The definition of *useful* is much more complex. For instance, many patents describe practical application areas and the advantages derived from using inventions without proving industrial producibility and cost effectiveness.

Patents are not granted if their subject matter has been described by others in any country, or has been disclosed or on sale in this country for more than one year.

The mechanism of patent protection begins with an application, containing specifications, drawings (optional), and one or more claims. Claims describe the specific protection that the inventors are seeking. In the specification, the inventors must recite the prior art of which they are aware, and explain each element claimed with enough details so that someone of ordinary skill in the art may reproduce the invention. Examples of ways to reduce the invention to practice are included in the specifications, but they do not restrict the protection coverage.

The patent examiners undertake searches of both issued patents and open literature and decide, for each application, whether one or more claims are valid. Then, they notify the inventors of the claims allowed. Allowance does not constitute protection; it merely indicates that protection is obtainable.

Up to this point, the applications and all related proceedings, including information of what claims have been allowed, are kept confidential. Upon notification of allowance the inventor has two options: to keep the information confidential and receive no protection, or to pay the final fee, in which case a patent is issued and all information on file becomes public.

In most cases inventors elect to have the patent issued; in some cases they interrupt the proceedings at this point and keep the information secret.

If the examiner rejects some or all claims, the inventors may argue the merit of that decision and have a limited right to introduce more evidence supporting the application. The inventors may also change the wording of certain claims—for instance, by narrowing the area covered—if the examiner indicates that such changes would make the claims allowable.

Patents may have value even though the inventor does not intend to manufacture and market the invention. Licensing agreements involving royalty payments can be negotiated based on patents; a tangible value can be attributed to patents in the case a company is acquired by another.

### Trade Secrets

Information concerning formulas, patterns, devices, or whatever else gives businesses or individuals an advantage over competitors who are not cognizant of such information is a trade secret. Diligence must be exercised to protect confidentiality, so that it would be difficult to acquire this information by legal means.

Essential features of trade secrets include the unavailability of similar information outside the business, the effort or money expended in developing the information, the extent to which the information is guarded, the value of the information to a business or its competitors, and the ease with which similar information could be independently acquired.

Reverse engineering—the learning of how a product was made by analyzing its components and surmising its manufacturing methods—is a legitimate practice that may negate trade secrets.

Protection of trade secrets is often effected by negotiating nondisclosure agreements with employees, consultants, and financial institutions.

## Trademarks and Servicemarks

Trademarks and servicemarks[3] include any word, symbol, device, or combination thereof used to distinguish a product from those manufactured or marketed by others.

A trademark or servicemark can be registered only when the name or sentence selected is distinctly different from names or sentences already registered. Registration affords added legal protection, such as the right to sue in federal courts and the possibility of recovering treble damage and costs. Registrations are granted by the Patent and Trademark Office of the U.S. Department of Commerce.

A trademark or servicemark prevents others from using the same expression in the identification of competitive products or services. To retain its value, a trademark or servicemark must be followed by the superscript [TM] or [SM], respectively. If registered, it must be followed by an encircled superscript [®]. Failure to do this will permit the trademark or servicemark to be accepted in common use, in which case its protective power is negated.

## Copyright

Copyright[4] protects literary, dramatic, musical, and artistic work from being copied without permission. A description of an invention can be copyrighted, but such protection concerns only the copying of the description, not the manufacture and marketing of the invention. Copyright gives its owner the exclusive right to prepare derivative work and, in the case of audiovisual works, to perform in public.

Material denied copyright protection includes works in the public domain; ideas, principles, and discoveries; works that do not require an appreciable amount of creative effort; work produced by government employees as a part of their normal duties; and devices or blank forms based on common ideas or methods.

Copyright is secured automatically when the work is created—that is, the work is fixed in a copy for the first time. Registration, granted by the United States Copyright Office, Library of Congress, affords additional protection, especially in case of litigation.

Notice should be given that a work is copyrighted, by using an encircled superscript ©, or the word "Copyright," followed by the year of first publication and the name of the owner of the copyright. The copyright owner is accorded exclusive rights to reproduce the work, prepare derivative work, distribute the work by selling, leasing, renting, or lending, and, in the case of literary, dramatic, or musical work, perform or display the work publicly.

Copyright protection is valid for at least 50 years.

### Foreign Protection

We have discussed protection laws in the United States. Today, protection in other countries is generally desirable. Each country has its own code, proceedings, and litigation rules. This is a very complex field of law and must be handled by a specialist.

In most countries patent protection requires the payment of yearly maintenance fees, which often increase during the life of the patent and become very substantial in the later years. Because of such fees, and because coverage is generally sought in more than one country, foreign protection is a very expensive proposition. As a part of the new product planning, consideration should be given to the extent of foreign protection needed to succeed in business. A realistic budget must include the costs of those proceedings.

### Litigation

Litigation may ensue even before protection is obtained; for instance, whenever, during patent proceedings, there appears to be interference between patent applications on similar subject matters; or when a trademark is denied because of its similarity to others that are already registered.

Most litigation concerns infringement; that is, illegal manufacture, marketing, publication, or performance of a protected work. Lawsuits have no prerequisites, but trademarks, servicemarks, and copyright registration at times facilitate the proceedings. Proprietary protection has little value if its owner does not have the means to sue for infringement.

## Principal Problems and Their Solutions

Many new product development teams have inadequate knowledge of laws and regulations. Thus, team members may unwittingly impair patent protection proceedings, for instance, by premature disclosure of information. Similar problems arise from inadequate diligence in keeping valid records during the development process. The establishment of the date when an invention was first conceived, reduced to practice, or revealed publicly is exceedingly important. Prompt indoctrination on record keeping of all new employees involved in new product development and periodic refresher sessions for older employees are essential.

Inadequate knowledge of prior art before and during development is another major problem. International patent searches can be carried out rapidly and at a minimum cost. They should be done and updated periodically. Open literature should also be perused periodically, keeping in mind the necessity of discriminating prior art from the invention sought. Note that prior art literature is often reviewed with emphasis on technical subject matter and marketing repercussions. Such literature must also be critically reviewed with focus on its interfering with the granting of proprietary protection.

Expert advice on patent application timing is critically needed. Timing may be premature because an issued patent can be cited by the examiner against a subsequent application for the protection of an improved product, if such improvement could be anticipated. Timing may also be premature when the lead time to full production and commercializations of a new product is very long. In this case, patents may expire before the end of the product life. On the other hand, to delay protection may give the competition the opportunity of preempting this privilege.

The wording of the patent claims is critical. A broad coverage is desirable, especially if it does not interfere with the opportunity of obtaining narrower and more specific coverages later on. Narrow coverages are easier to obtain, but can also be circumvented more readily by the competition.

Generally, a single patent offers little protection and has limited value for licensing, acquisitions, or joint venture negotiations, unless it is based on a major technical breakthrough. Companies intending to become well established in a new product line should seek a network of patents and other proprietary protections, acquired year after year.

Proprietary protection must be planned along with the business, technical, and commercial aspects of new product development.

## Example

We shall exemplify proprietary protection by analyzing U.S. Patent 2,158,130. This is one of numerous patents based on inventions by Edwin H. Land and assigned to the Polaroid Corporation. (In Chapter 13, we shall give a historical synopsis of the outstanding new product development record of that inventor and that corporation.). The title is "Light Polarizer," the application date July 16, 1938 and the issue date May 16, 1939. It contains eight claims.

The introduction first describes the subject matter: "This invention relates to a new and improved light-polarizer, and more particularly to a polarizer adapted to resolve an incident beam. . . . "

The following paragraphs outline the purpose of the invention: "An object of the invention is to provide a light-polarizer of the character described. . . . Another object. . . . Other objects. . . . "

The specification then states that the invention comprises an article of manufacture possessing certain unique " . . . features, properties, and the relation of elements which will be exemplified in the article hereinafter described, and the scope of the application of which will be indicated in the claims."

The inventor has stated that, in his opinion, the product is new, useful, and constructed with special materials and in a special way. This statement sets the stage for describing one way of reducing invention to practice: "Hence a preferred embodiment of the invention is one employing rod-shaped or needle-shaped crystals, as crystals of this form are easily oriented." The inventor carefully notes that other embodiments and materials are also viable. A drawing adds to the clarity of the description of the invention.

The front part of the patent (the so-called specification) does not afford protection. It is there to support the claims that follow. Only the claims describe what is protected by the patent. Skillful wording of the claims is critical.

This patent has these eight claims:

"1. A light polarizer adapted to . . . comprising a plurality of sheet-like suspensions . . . the particles of one medium being oriented. . . . " What is claimed is an article of commerce, useful in given applications, and manufactured with materials having given characteristics.

"2. In combination, a suspension of oriented needle-shaped, birifringent particles, having. . . . " The construction of the article is further described in detail. The more specific is such description, the less likely that alternative ways of practicing the invention by a competitor could be designed.

"3. In combination, a plurality of suspensions . . . one of said suspensions comprising . . . and having an index of refraction . . . , the other suspension comprising . . . and means to superimpose said suspensions so that the direction. . . . " This claim extends the coverage from an article composed of the material described in claim 2, to an article composed of several layers of materials having the features described in claim 2 but differing in their construction and performance.

"4. In combination, a suspension of oriented needle-shaped particles of barium carbonate in a light transmitting medium having . . . said suspension being superimposed. . . . " The generic description of the article is further narrowed by specifying a material (barium carbonate) which has appropriate characteristics.

"5. In combination, a suspension of oriented needle-shaped particles of urea...." An alternative material is here specified.

"6. In combination, a suspension ... the index of refraction ... and a second suspension ... overlaying said first suspension and positioned to intercept light...." A two-layer article is described, precisely specifying the relations between the optical properties of the various components and the relation between the two layers.

"7. A light-polarizer comprising a plurality of suspensions...." The invention is here described as a useful article of commerce: a light-polarizer. The specific characteristics that make this article useful, in terms of materials and construction, are reiterated.

"8. Means interposed in the path of a beam of non-polarized light for resolving said beam into two components..., said means comprising a suspension ... and a second suspension...." The characteristics of the invention are again reiterated, but from the viewpoint of their ultimate function. In so doing, coverage is effectively extended to *alternative ways of practicing the invention* that can be anticipated by those skilled in the art.

The inventor has described the new product both in generic and in specific terms, has outlined the method of manufacture, and has stated the useful performance features of his invention. He has given examples of materials that could be used to practice the invention, without limiting his claims to these materials. He has claimed means of achieving a useful function by practicing the invention. The example given in the specification strongly supports the claims and suggests alternative ways of practicing the invention. This is a strong patent, but it is only one of many. The resulting patent network constitutes a defense that is difficult to pierce.

## Conclusions

New product development should be regarded as an investment; protection of this intangible asset is in order. United States laws offer several means of protecting new products and services, comprising patents, trademarks or servicemarks, and copyright. Patents grant a limited monopoly in exchange for the publication of the information on which they are based. Inventors can, however, maintain this information confidential as trade secrets, in which case patent protection cannot be obtained.

The field of proprietary protection is highly specialized and the consequence of improprieties are very severe. Hence specialists must be engaged to assure that proceedings are properly executed and appropriate timing selected.

Patent protection is most effective if a network of patents is created, so that ways of circumventing proprietary fences are difficult to find. Such networks must be planned in advance, and should include, besides patents, copyrights and trademarks.

All personnel engaged in new product development should be appropriately indoctrinated in the essential features of proprietary protection when they are first employed, and periodically thereafter. These indoctrinations stimulate sensitivity to issues that are not of natural concern to most technical and commercial developers. The appointment of liaison persons, who bridge the gap between members of the development team and legal advisors, is highly desirable. Of special importance is the indoctrination about record keeping.

Proprietary protection abroad is difficult and expensive; yet it must be considered seriously because of the international nature of most manufacturing and marketing operations.

Infringement proceedings are likewise very time consuming and expensive. Thus, new product planning must include enough human and financial resources to properly protect this intangible investment.

## Notes

The author is indebted to George Grayson, Esq. for his helpful comments on this chapter.

1. United States *Constitution,* Bill of Rights, Article 1, Section 8.

2. Jeffrey M. Samuels, Ed., *Patent, Trademark and Copyright Law*, 1985 Edition (Washington, DC: The Bureau of National Affairs, Inc., 1985).

3. United States, Department of Commerce, Patent and Trademark Office, *Basic Facts about Trademarks*, Revised (Washington, DC: U.S. Government Printing Office, August 1988).

4. United States, Library of Congress, Copyright Office, *Copyright Basics*, Circular 1 (Washington, DC: U.S. Government Printing Office, 1988).

**PART IV**

# WHO?—THE HUMAN SIDE

# 11

# Organization

## Introduction

Management science literature on organizational schemes abounds, but nowhere can one find a challenge to the need for an organization. The independent entrepreneurs who create with their own hands do not need one, just as an amoeba does not need more than one cell, let alone functionally specialized organs. The successful entrepreneurs hire helpers; initially everybody knows who the boss is. An organization as we understand it is not needed. Eventually a third layer is interposed between the boss and the workers. The third layer consists of sector managers—persons whose primary responsibilities are to see that the job is done in specific business areas rather than doing it themselves.

The organization that prevails in enterprises that employ more than a handful of people essentially derives from a primitive three-layer structure that is expanded horizontally and vertically. Horizontal expansion signifies increasing the number of sectors, such as marketing, finances, public relations, and human resources. Vertical expansion signifies adding more organizational layers between the general manager and the lowest level workers. Eventually such expansions create communication and other problems that are usually solved by superimposing another organization onto the principal one. Such solutions often create more problems than they cure.

This chapter will describe the principal schemes of complex organizations, their strengths and their weaknesses. The organization of the new product development function will be framed within that of a profit center. Then the specific requirements of technical and commercial development organizations will be highlighted, and the all-important role of the top management emphasized.

Organizational schemes are as old as human civilization; references thereto can be found in the Bible and in other ancient writings. These schemes are here to stay, but will evolve as technological progress will require more rapid decisions about more complex situations. Management techniques, helped by high-power computers, will also evolve. Fundamentally, however, the basic principles will not change.

The most important principle of organizations is that *responsibilities* can be delegated but *accountabilities* cannot. Managers can select to do a job themselves or ask their reportees to carry out some tasks. In either case they are accountable for the outcome of the actions of everyone concerned with their operations.

Organization charts and other descriptions should not be confused with the actual functioning of an enterprise. Drivers planning a cross-country trip carefully map their routing; but, as obstacles materialize, the routes are adjusted. So it is for organizations. They are supposed to work in certain ways; as need arises, long lines are short circuited and new connections made. Moreover, certain individuals within the organizations gain unappointed power, while others do not exert the power that is invested in them. Understanding the real organization is more important than the perusal of the organization chart.

## Organization of a Profit Center

Mergers and acquisitions have created business enterprises of enormous complexity. In many cases the parent corporation is but a holding company—it owns all the shares of all operating subsidiaries. It does not manufacture or sell products and therefore is not directly involved with new product development. A holding company is essentially an asset manager. It buys, sells, divides, merges, and restructures operating companies.

An operating company, whether independent or owned by a parent corporation, is often subdivided into profit centers, which may be more or less independent of each other and of the parent corporation. In this case the extent to which the new product development process is centralized or decentralized varies.

To be profitable, an organization must be able to produce, sell, and maintain in the long run a favorable relation between costs and revenues and a working capital sufficient to dampen the fluctuating cash flow.

A profit center must have a general manager, often called president or chief executive officer, who has *full profit accountability*. If the profit center is an independent corporation or an incorporated subsidiary, the general manager reports to the board of directors, which represents the stockholders. One of the prime responsibilities of the board of directors is to appoint the general manager.

The general manager has a number of reportees, each charged with well defined responsibilities *and accountabilities*. Management science often distinguishes between reportees having *line* and *staff* functions—line signifying *executive* responsibilities for vital portions of the enterprise such as manufacturing and marketing; staff signifying *advisory* responsibilities concerning auxiliary functions such as planning, public relations, and human resources. In effect, all line managers also fulfill staff functions because they act as advisors to their superiors. Staff managers may carry line functions, often by special assignments. For instance, a planning manager may be assigned the additional duty of acting as general manager of a product line that has yet to reach full commercialization.

Multidivisional corporations may have line managers at each profit center assisted by a staff manager at the parent corporation level. Even some of the staff functions may have managers at each profit center and at the parent corporation levels. These complexities seldom arise in enterprises that consist of a single profit center. In larger, more diversified enterprises responsibilities and accountabilities must be defined in such a way as to create no ambiguities.

Some organizations solve the problems that arise from their complexity by adopting the so-called matrix schemes. According to these schemes, the chief executive officer has two sets or reportees; one concerns *functions* such as manufacturing, marketing, engineering, finance, and human resources, the other concerns *missions* or *strategic business units*. Nearly all activities of the profit centers are controlled by two executives; one is primarily responsible for the professional standards and the efficiency of a function, the other for the achievement of the mission objectives. J. H. Sheridan[1] offered a simplified description of the matrix organization and its functioning.

One of the important issues of all complex organizations is the degree of centralization. This issue has major repercussions on the organization and functioning of the new product development process.

## The Organization of the New Product Development Process

We shall make the simplifying assumption that all new product development activities are carried out in-house. As previously explained, a variable fraction thereof is farmed out. This state of affairs does not affect organizational schemes other than creating the need for appointing liaison personnel.

The selection of a new product development organization is critical and depends on several factors; the corporate culture and philosophy and the personality of the chief executive officer are of utmost importance. Other critical factors depend on the principal objective of new product development. Such objective may consist of a major diversification, the development of a new product line complementary to an existing one, the adaptation of a current product to new markets, and the improvement of current products for current customers.

The above-mentioned factors determine the most effective degree of centralization. The two extreme choices are to centralize all activities at the corporate level, led by an executive reporting to the corporate president, and to subdivide all activities into a number of independent organizational units, each reporting to the head of a profit center or to a product manager.

When major diversification is not the principal objective, the organization of the new product development function is usually a part of the profit center that manufactures and markets similar products. In the case of a major diversification, new product development is best carried out by a cost center, such as a planning corporate department, detached from all profit centers.

Organizational decisions should not be confused with funding choices. For instance, new product development may be implemented within a profit center, but funded by another, or by the parent corporation, or by multiple sources.

## Technical Development Organization

In Chapter 8 the distinction was made between activities aimed at defining business objectives (exploratory R&D) and activities aimed at fulfilling well-defined business objectives (project R&D). This distinction needs not, and usually should not, be paralleled by a similar dichotomy in the organization. The organizational intermixing of personnel assigned to exploratory and project R&D is constructive, as long as funding policies are not compromised and managerial practices recognize the need for different styles and interpretation of administrative rules.

## Need for Establishing and Maintaining a Capability

Technical organizations should be designed to construct and preserve technical capabilities. A capability is not merely a combination of facilities and trained specialists; it includes an appropriate balance of skills, supporting services, and direction. The selection of personnel could be equated to the casting of a play. First a script must be prepared. This corresponds to the program plan of technical development. The cast of characters is chosen based on this plan and the cast is then selected.

This simile holds up to a point. In the performing arts, the script leaves little leeway for changes, whereas a program plan has a degree of flexibility. On the other hand, the performing arts have more flexibility with regard to casting. Different actors can be chosen for different performances. A technical capability has much less flexibility in this respect, because personnel expansions and curtailments and changes in styles of direction cannot be achieved without turmoil.

### Skills and Missions

One of the principal problems confronting a technical organization is the need to maintain specialized technical *skills* while fulfilling at the same time certain well-defined *missions* that require multidisciplinary teams. Technical specialists feel most comfortable when they are surrounded by peers and have the opportunity of improving their skills while discharging their duties. Managers responsible for missions want to achieve integration and the functional application of adequate, but not necessarily elegant, technology. Conflicts arise in this respect. Conflicts also arise from cultural differences between scientists and engineers, and between technical- and business-oriented personnel.

These conflicts and related problems can be solved by appropriate organizational schemes. One of the more successful schemes is the establishment of skilled groups comprising personnel assigned to both exploratory and project R&D. The leader of each group is a well-recognized expert in a specific skill areas. Whenever a project must be organized, a temporary team is set up by extracting technical specialists from the various skill groups, and a project manager appointed. Such a manager could be a full-time person, specifically assigned to this duty, or any member of the permanent organization acting in a dual function.

An example will clarify this organizational concept. A company that produces and markets medical instrumentation, such as blood gas analyzers, wants to expand its product line to industrial analytical instruments. It has a technical organization comprising three principal skill groups: *chemistry*, *electronics*, and *materials*, plus a technical support group. Because the new product is technically akin to the current products, technical development is implemented within the profit center.

For the development of this new product the skills available are deficient because they do not include *industrial engineering*. This skill area is not needed in the case of medical instrumentation, because the product is standing alone and is generally operated by well-trained specialists. In a case of an industrial instrument, the product is generally inserted in a complex engineered system, such as a petroleum refinery or a power plant, and may be operated by personnel having limited training; therefore, it must be designed with these application features in mind.

A new skill group—industrial engineering—is created. Because the compatibility with the customers' systems is critical, the head of the industrial engineering group is also appointed project manager. Team members are selected from the four skill groups and a new mission-oriented capability is so formed.

## Regeneration of a Technical Capability

Organizational dislocations often arise whenever a new product development project is started and a new multidisciplinary team is formed. For instance, some technical experts may not be needed as members of the new project team. Unless they can be gainfully attached to preexisting project teams, they should be redeployed to exploratory R&D until such time as they are needed for future projects.

When the new project has been successfully completed, some team members are likely to be transferred to newly created positions outside the technical organization. This creates other organizational dislocations.

These dislocations must be promptly cured in order to maintain an effective technical capability. The *self-regeneration* of technical organizations is a necessary ingredient of success in the long run.

### Issues, Problems, and Their Solutions

At this point the reader may wonder how we could have talked about organizations without sketching pictures containing many boxes. This omission is intentional. It serves to emphasize that technical personnel do not like to be fenced into boxes. The more inflexibly the functioning organization adheres to a preset scheme, the less creativity it is likely to have.

Technical development organizations must allow team members to interact with potential users of new products without interfering with the policies and plans designed by the commercial development organization. Excessive sheltering or excessive freedom can lead to severe problems that may impair the ultimate outcome of the joint effort.

Another potential problem area may develop when the new product is about to move from the laboratory or pilot plant to commercial production. There must be continuity, without excessive interference by the technical team with those responsible for fully developing industrial producibility.

## Commercial Development Organization

Some of the concepts and issues enunciated in the previous section, such as choices of centralization and the need to preserve a self-regenerating capability, apply to commercial as well as to technical organizations. Others are specific. For instance, a well-staffed marketing organization is capable of carrying out effective commercial development of new products following various organizational schemes; a sales department is seldom well-equipped to do this. The objective of a sales organization is always to sell; the objective of a commercial development organization is often to determine to whom, when, and how to market a new product. A sales organization is given well-defined descriptions of the specification and applications of a product line that can be routinely produced; a commercial development organization must consider how to adapt or improve the new products and continuously searches for new applications. A sales organization primarily influences buyers; a commercial development organization must influence engineers, while keeping harmonious relations with buyers. Finally, a sales organization is always concerned about the competition between a new product and current products. A certain degree of conflict of interests usually prevails.

When diversification is the primary objective, commercial development is generally implemented within newly created profit centers. When the new product is a modification or adaptation of a current product, commercial development is implemented within an established profit center, and utilizes members of the marketing department of that profit center.

The transition from early commercial to full commercial status is critical, because during this transition new products are most vulnerable.

The commercial development of new products is often farmed out, at least in part; for instance, when a joint venture is involved, or when the new product is expected to be marketed through a distributor. The third party is likely to become a partner during the early commercialization phase; thus the internal commercial development organization must take into consideration the need for appropriate liaison and joint decision making.

## Top Management Issues

The selected organizational structure, its staffing and administrative policies, and the availability of support services greatly influence the degree of success of the new product development process. However, by far the principal success factor is the role that top management plays. Without *sustained* support by top management, the new product development process is likely to wither or to go astray.

Top management has three basic responsibilities:

- Define the corporate environment and objectives.
- Establish ultimate goals and realistic expectations.
- Control the new product development process.

The captain of a merchant ship is charged with delivering a cargo from the United States to a remote station in Antarctica. The captain knows the ultimate objective, but must also understand the limitation of the environment and the capabilities of the ship, which in turn determine what specific goals are realistic. For instance, passage is possible only within a time window; the cargo cannot be unloaded in the remote station as fast as in a well-equipped harbor; speed must be decreased as the destination is approached; allowance must be made for storms that may delay the journey. Even though the crew is well trained and supervised, the captain must periodically establish the ship location, steer the course as needed, see that illnesses and stresses have not affected the human resources, watch for other vessels that may intersect the ship route—in other words, *control* unrelentlessly.

What are the most common problems caused by inadequate top management performance and what consequences derive from them?

### Ill-defined Assignments and Accountabilities

By nature, the new product development process cannot have all detailed goals, modes of operation, and timing exactly defined. This limitation must be compensated by seeing that the roles of all team members are well defined, and accountabilities of leaders established *and publicized*. There is no time to be wasted in searching for who can make which decision. There is no room for gaps in responsibilities. There is no chance that success can be reached if responsibilities overlap and leaders give contradictory directives. Top management must see that functions are clearly spelled out, appointments clearly defined, and conflicts promptly resolved.

### Late or Erratic Involvement

All too often top management becomes involved in new product development only when it becomes aware of critical events, such as a budget overrun, overall economic stresses, and pressure from the board of directors. This kind of management by crisis is devastating. Worse yet is top management's lack of attention to embryonic projects that use limited resources, and march on course. Involvement must not be erratic.

Top management can establish periodic reviews or informal visits with team members from time to time; in any event there must be continuity and personal involvement. Monthly reports should not be one-way streets. Even when returned with evidence that they passed by the chief executive's desk, they give little support to team members. Questions do much to challenge people and make them feel important. Suggestions for alternative approaches, on the other hand, should be handled with care and always transmitted through appropriate channels.

### Too Much Permissiveness

Even though top management is often criticized for exerting too much pressure on the organization, very often budget overruns, delays in goal achievements, organizational problems, inability to staff appropriately, and other substandard performances are not challenged by top management, at least until these problems generate a crisis situation. Constructive criticism is welcomed by all responsible workers. Neglect, especially when team members are conscious of their inadequate performance, generates negative reactions which may range from insecurity in the more responsible fraction of the staff, to the attitude of "see what I can get away with" in others. Standards of performance must be established and adhered to.

### Inadequate Integration of Functions

One of the principal duties of top management is to integrate the various functions that the enterprise needs for achieving success. Such integration is much more critical in new product development than in other operational sectors. The integration of technical and commercial development is a case in point. Integration of the new and the old is another case. Only the destiny planner can exercise judgment in this regard and has the necessary executive power. Lack of integration generates not only morale problems but also wastes energy and time. At worst, inadequate integration may undermine the stability of the business based on current products.

### Too Much Emphasis on the Short Term

This is the most common complaint heard in new product development organizations. To a certain extent, it derives from the practice of changing executives, by promotion, dismissal, or voluntary resignation, at time intervals that are shorter than the average time needed to achieve success in new product development. The executives who know that their positions will probably change within five years are unlikely to place much emphasis on projects that have a lead time of ten years. Even if these situations do not prevail, emphasis on the short term may be prompted by contingent economic pressures, incentive policies that reward short-term performance, and other factors.

## Example of an Organizational Scheme

Precision Electronics (a fictitious enterprise bearing no relation to any company having a similar name) is a public corporation with a revenue of about 100 million dollars and good profitability. Its product lines consist of surgical laser systems, data processing equipment for medical laboratories, hospital communication systems, and electronic intrusion detection systems. The company is organized as indicated in the simplified organization chart of Figure 11.1. There are two profit centers, one (medical) responsible for the first three product lines, the other (security) for the other. Each profit center has two or three new products under development, one of which, in the security division, is close to being commercialized and concerns car theft detection.

The financial control and all supporting services are centralized. Operations, marketing, and technology are decentralized. New product development is planned and implemented only within each division.

The president, assisted by a strategic consultant and a staff assistant, determines that the company should add a third profit center. After considering several options, the president's office concludes that the third center will capitalize on frontier technology and have an outstanding long-term potential even at the risk of impairing short-term profits. In order to defuse possible negative reactions from the personnel of the two operating divisions, the president appoints a committee comprising members of staff departments and of the two divisions, charging it to select the new business and develop a preliminary plan.

The committee chooses microelectromechanical devices as the new product line. These are functioning machines, such as motors and gears, that are only

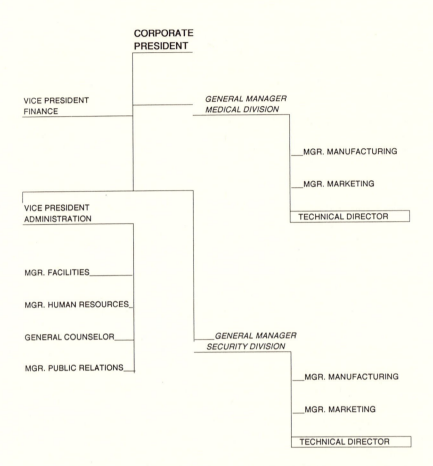

Figure 11.1 Organization of Precision Electronics (a fictitious company): Technology Is Decentralized

a fraction of an inch in size. They are fabricated primarily by microelectronic technologies—those used for producing integrated circuits—a technical skill area in which the company does not have adequate know-how.

The president's office, confronted with the decision of developing the new product line in house or to acquire an emerging company in this technical area, opts for the second and acquires an enterprise that has negligible revenue, but excellent long-term potential. How should the new product development be organized?

One obvious choice is to establish the newly acquired company as a third profit center, charged with full responsibility for product development. Another choice is to divide the corporation into a "today" and a "tomorrow" branch; the first led by an executive vice-president to whom the general managers of the medical and security division report; and the second led by the former president of the acquired company. A third choice is to centralize technology at the corporate level, charging it with responsibility for all new product development. According to this scheme, the preexisting divisions and the new division maintain only a minimal engineering and customer support staff, but implement the commercial development of the new products originating from the corporate technology organization.

The president's office decides to select the third choice, because it promotes integration of technical skills and minimize excessive emphasis on the short-term. Because the newly-established corporate technology must serve present and future needs, the matrix organization displayed in Figure 11.2 is adopted.

## History of Industrial Technical Organizations

Industrial research laboratories and other technical organizations as we understand them today did not exist one hundred years ago. Technical development was principally implemented within manufacturing departments. We review the origin of two outstanding industrial research laboratories and determine to which extent their original concept, function, and structure is still valid.

### The General Electric Laboratory[2]

Dr. Arthur Buche, one of the giants of American technology management, admonished that the concern of R&D is the future, not the past. Yet, he added, from time to time it is wise to pause and look back.

At the turn of the century, the enormous business potential of electric power was obvious to all, but the value of industrial research laboratories was not. The concept of a central technical organization did not exist. At the General Electric Company, this concept emerged from a discussion between a consultant and three employees; an electrical engineer, a vice-president, and a patent attorney. The vice-president and the consultant jointly decided how to flesh out this concept. They first selected the director—a young, imaginative chemistry professor, Willis Rodney Whitney of the Massachusetts Institute of Technology. Then they chose the facilities—a barn in a private estate. Initially, the newly-appointed director served on a part-time basis, commuting by train weekly from Boston to Schenectady. It was the year 1901.

Many received this new organization with skepticism. These unimaginative critics thought that materials to produce electric energy superior to copper, carbon, and iron could never be found.

The laboratory developed and grew during the ensuing years and eventually moved from the original barn to an unimpressive building situated in the middle of the General Electric plant. Here the first market need was identified and became the goal of the first new product development project. Electric light had many advantages over gas and other alternatives, but the life of the earliest

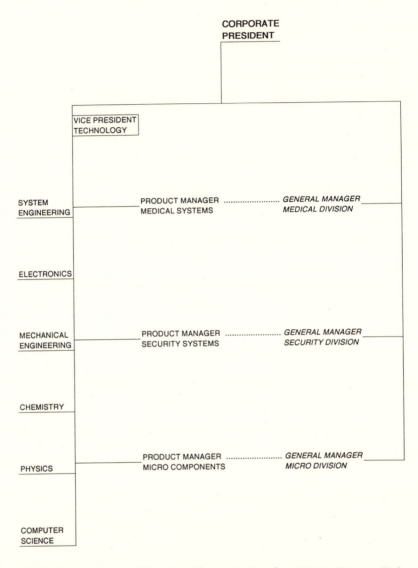

Figure 11.2  Reorganization of Precision Electronics Based on Matrix Concept: Technology Is Centralized

light bulbs, which had a carbon filament, was too short. This made electric lighting too costly and impaired its growth.

The researchers identified tungsten as the potentially perfect material for the electric bulb filaments. Tungsten could stand high temperatures and emit brilliant light but had inadequate life because it was too brittle. The researchers realized that, whereas carbon—the filament of the Edison bulb—is inherently brittle, tungsten is not. Thus, the technical problem definition changed from the search for a new product to the search for an enabling process technology, a very common event in new product development.

The development team was convinced that the goal was achievable given enough time, effort, and ingenuity. The effort was crowned by success six years later and the tungsten bulb became a commercial reality shortly thereafter. Credit for this invention is mainly given to William D. Coolidge who had founded the General Electric Company laboratory, a wonderful place to work because the director had "successfully transplanted a lot of academic atmosphere."

The first major improvement of the original tungsten bulb was implemented by Irving Langmuir. Not resting on prior achievements, researchers sought ways of further improving electric bulb life which was known to be a function of the quality of the vacuum inside the bulb. Having realized that a higher vacuum quality was difficult to achieve, Langmuir banked on "bad vacuum" as he called an oxygen-free atmosphere. He filled the bulb with a gas such as nitrogen or argon, thereby increasing life by several hundred fold. The year was 1910.

The technical team proceeded to improve radio and x-ray tubes. Then the team moved from better ways of *utilizing* electric energy to better ways of *generating* it. In 1919 the General Engineering Laboratory was created. By 1935 a substantial fraction of the technical effort was devoted to electronics, telecommunication equipment, and industrial control. By 1940 a new product line, the silicones, approached commercial feasibility, and from there, toward synthetic diamonds, nuclear energy, high performance polymers.

The General Electric Company, by way of innovations and judicious acquisitions, grew to be a multinational, 50-billion dollar enterprise. Generation and utilization of electric energy are still the major foundations of its business goals.

During its first seventy-five years and beyond, the General Electric Laboratory went through changes in direction, size, organization. It is still one of the most stable and productive industrial technical establishments. What can we learn from its early history and successes?

We can learn that beginnings may be modest, facilities may be limited, technical problems may be arduous, but with skill, courage, and determination realistic technical and business goals can be achieved. We can learn that the success of research and development operations is often dependent on the creativity and technical knowledge of one or a few team members. We can learn about the importance of a stimulating environment, the invaluable power of good direction and top management support. And we can learn that progress in the application of electric energy can be achieved by chemists, not only by physicists and electrical engineers; labeling technical personnel does not improve their know-how or creativity.

### Eastman Kodak Research Laboratories

The General Electric Laboratory was well established, but still of very modest proportions when George Eastman recognized the need for a similar organization. He had been mainly impressed by the research laboratories he had seen in Germany in 1911. His new product development dream was color photography.

As in the previous example, the first step was to search for a laboratory director. C E K Mees, then a 27-year old, was working for a small firm in England and had achieved an outstanding reputation with his doctoral thesis on the theory of the photographic process. He was finding the small firm environment too confining and gladly accepted the opportunity of moving to Rochester to create a new industrial research laboratory.

Mees left us a very valuable heritage: a book,[3] first published in 1920, on the organization and management of industrial research laboratories. This book is well worth reading seventy years later. It shows how many concepts and principles of technical development are still valid. Mees emphasized the need for segregating activities according to their objectives, thereby sheltering a function from the encroachments by others. The three principal functions were defined as improvement of operation and attendant cost reduction, development of new products and processes, and development of fundamental theories. Mees was most emphatic on the need for long-term, scientific research, well sheltered from short-term business pressures.

Mees recognized the value of the few, exceptional researchers who, from time to time, appeared and achieved great feats, but admonished that progress mainly depends on more ordinary people. He wrote, "men who are only average when dealt with singly may become extremely able by mental contact which follows association with other men working on similar problems." The synergistic effects of team effort were thus highlighted.

Mees also recognized the need for flexibility in research laboratories. "In the organization of a laboratory it is essential to take into account the peculiarities of the individuals who compose it." His classic book continues by discussing freedom of choice, remuneration, facilities and equipment, budgeting, research direction, and program selection.

The history of new product development at Eastman Kodak[4] up to the sixties is summarized in Table 11.1. The original product line—photographic goods—generated the need to develop special chemicals. These special chemicals, in turn, generated opportunities for businesses based on chemical goods. This process, what we shall call *vector growth*, is one of the most powerful ways of capitalizing on technical developments.

A pioneering concept at Eastman Kodak was, and still is, the dependence on an international character. This concept affected technical activities as well as business. As this company sought foreign markets, technical activities were internationalized by implementing some of them in many countries, in asso-

## Table 11.1.
## History of Product Development at Eastman Kodak, 1890–1970

| DECADE ENDING | PHOTOGRAPHIC GOODS | CHEMICAL GOODS |
|---|---|---|
| 1890 | PROFESSIONAL PLATES | |
| 1900 | FLEXIBLE BASE PROFESSIONAL MOVIES | |
| 1910 | RADIOLOGY PRODUCTS | |
| 1920 | | SYNTHETIC ORGANIC CHEMICALS |
| 1930 | AMATEUR MOVIES MICROFILMS | |
| 1940 | COLOR TRANSPARENCIES | CELLULOSE ACETATE DYES |
| 1950 | OFFICE COPIERS COLOR NEGATIVE FILM | SYNTHETIC VITAMIN A |
| 1960 | AUTOMATIC CAMERA | TENITE POLYETHYLENE KODEL, VEREL FIBERS |
| 1970 | PHOTO INSTRUMENTATION SUPER-8 MOVIES | POLYALLOMER DYES FOR POLYESTER |

Source: Hanson, W.T.J. "Research at Kodak." *British Journal of Photography* 116, (1969), 8–11, 13.

ciation with foreign manufacturing subsidiaries. Each technical center had a substantial degree of autonomy, but was coordinated with the others in order to gain overall effectiveness.

The General Electric and the Eastman Kodak histories show parallelism and differences. The major common bases of these two success stories are the convictions and unrelenting support of top management, and the guidance of outstanding technical directors. Other commonalities derive from dependence on a diversified staff, respect for individual preferences of environment and managerial styles, and focus on well defined business objectives.

## Conclusions

New product development organizations can be based on a variety of schemes, depending on the complexity of their operations, principal business goals, and top management style. Accordingly, they can be more or less decentralized, and could consist of a matrix whereby leadership is gained from experts in different skill areas as well as from managers responsible for the fulfillment of well defined missions.

Whereas many organizational principles apply to both technical and commercial organizations, some issues and problems affect primarily one of the two. The most important issue concerning technical development organization is the need to blend many specialized skills while focusing on a single ultimate objective. Because technical development constitutes a search for the unknown, and because of the need for homogenizing a diversified team, direction is most critical. The most important issue concerning commercial development organizations is the potential conflict between current and new products and the inadequacy of many sales organization. Other problems arise from excessive domination of the technical developers in the commercialization of new products and, at the other extreme, excessive detachment.

For all activities, the role of top management is very critical. Late and erratic involvement, hazy definitions of assignments and accountabilities, and too much emphasis on the short-term are a few shortcoming of marginal top management.

Whatever organization schemes are chosen, all personnel involved in new product development must understand the actual functioning of the organization, which often deviates substantially from what is graphically displayed on paper.

## Notes

1. J. H. Sheridan, "Matrix Maze. Are two bosses better than one?" *Industry Week*, 201 (June 11, 1979): 76–79.

2. General Electric Company, *GE R&D. The First Seventy-Five Years* (Schenectady, New York: General Electric Company, 1975).

3. C. E. Kenneth Mees, *The Organization of Industrial Scientific Research*, 1st Edition (New York, New York: McGraw-Hill Book Company, 1920).

4. W. T. Hanson Jr, "Research at Kodak." *The British Journal of Photography*, 116 (3 January 1969): 8–11, 13.

# 12

---

# Communication

## Introduction

Communication is defined in Webster's as "a process by which meanings are exchanged." Communication is not a sudden happening, but a *process*, something that develops continuously as it is going on. Communication is not a one-way street, but an *exchange* between two or more parties, something that involves interactions. Communication would fall short of its goal if it did not transmit the *meaning* of a message, rather than simply a statement.

In new product development, effective communication, so defined, is one of the most important success factors. However, failures are often attributed to poor communication when the actual cause of the problem is the failure to follow up promptly and effectively after a communication.

We shall highlight primarily the concepts enunciated by L. D. Thayer[1] because they principally concern the organizational environment.

We shall first distinguish between various types of communication, and then describe effective and ineffective modes. Problems and their solutions will be highlighted. The balance of this chapter will be devoted to mechanisms of information retrieval.

## Types of Communication

Thayer defines three fundamental types of communication:

- interpersonal
- organizational
- institutional

Interpersonal communication concerns the exchange of information between two or more individuals. In new product development it occurs frequently as an exchange between two individuals and in group meetings. The individuals involved may or may not belong to the same organization. Most often they do not; hence interpersonal communication may have an organi-

zational connotation whenever the individuals speak on behalf of their organizations rather than for themselves.

In new product development it is essential to communicate the business objectives, the desired goals, the roles of the various team players, the financial
and other repercussions of success and failures, legal issues, and much more.
Communication may occur in a structured fashion through organizational
lines as well as through informal channels, the latter often being the most
significant.

People cannot communicate effectively unless they speak the same language. By language we mean not only the tongue of different nationals, but
also the vernacular of different people speaking the same tongue. For instance,
*pig* means an animal to a farmer, but a cast piece of metal to a steel metallurgist. This metallurgist calls *foundry* a rather dirty shop where molten metal is
poured in a mold, whereas a microelectronic engineer calls foundry the ultra-
clean shop in which integrated circuits are fabricated.

Language issues, as defined above, also arise when technical and non-tech-
nical people communicate, and, at times, during interactions between scientists and engineers. In these cases, problems are primarily caused by the points
of view of the sender and of the receiver.

Organizational communication concerns the formal communicative interactions between organized groups within the same enterprise. Much information is procedural in nature; it may define authorities and responsibilities,
need to submit reports, ways of requesting allocations. In new product development, critical organizational communications are likely to arise between
technology and marketing groups, and between technology and manufacturing groups. For instance, a manufacturing department may want to define its
capabilities, a marketing department may recommend sites for field testing of
new products, and a technology department may request specific assistance
from the other two groups in order to better plan its activities.

Institutional communication concerns interactions between two or more
enterprises or between a company and a government agency, or between a
company and the customers at large. Public relation is, of course, effected by
way of institutional communication. In product development, institutional
communication is critical with regard to company positioning (see Chapter
9). The image that an enterprise succeeds in building is often a major success
factor in commercial development of new products.

Communication can be implemented through different media. The choice
of medium should be guided by assessments of effectiveness and propriety. In
interpersonal relations, verbal communication is generally most appropriate,
but can be affected by semantic, psychological, and other problems. Hence one
must verify that the meaning of the message has been comprehended. For this
reason, interpersonal communication should include test questions, or other
means to ascertain what has been received. Moreover, for best effectiveness,
the sender should always enunciate messages from the receiver's viewpoint.

This is especially important when communication occurs between people at different organizational levels.

For example, the general manager of an entrepreneurial company has been approached by a larger company concerning a potential strategic partnership. The status of a new product development project is critical and must be ascertained promptly and accurately. The general manager needs to personally assess the probability of success and the severity and nature of roadblocks, some of which may be removed by the potential partner. Dependence on periodic progress reports is not effective, and dependence on the sole opinion of the project manager is risky. The general manager decides to talk on a one-to-one basis with three key team members, but carefully avoids reference to the potential joint venture. Rather, the three key team members are asked about the status of the project *from their viewpoints*. Do they have adequate support? Are they satisfied with the progress? What could accelerate progress? Can the general manager help them in any way to achieve their goals? Should the initial emphasis have been placed on the negative effects of a project failure on the pending joint venture (the *general manager's viewpoint*) interpersonal communication would have been severely impaired.

Interpersonal communication can be effected through written media, but caution should be exercised; the written medium is excellent for broadcasting general information in a uniform way to a large audience. It is often effective in establishing the status of a project, in commending a job well done (generating something that people can show to their spouses or friends), and in communicating procedures. The written medium is damaging whenever it entails a request that can more effectively be made verbally, thus giving the receiver an opportunity to comment on it before taking action. It is devastating when it entails the censuring of a faulty performance except in cases where the written medium is mandatory for legal or contractual reasons.

Organizational communications are, on the other hand, best effected by written media (including electronic mail).

Institutional communication must select the best medium on a contingent basis. Media range from group conferences to television advertising, from brochures to letters to the editors of periodicals. Videotapes often are an excellent medium, perhaps not exploited to the extent of their potential. Since the majority of households are today equipped with videorecorders, a short tape handed to an influential party may be viewed in a quiet hour at home, and its message more readily accepted than a message delivered during business hours.

## Modes of Communication

Thayer defines four modes of communication as a way of emphasizing the most serious problems that may arise in communicative systems concerning organizations:

- Parallel—The information is transmitted from a sender to a receiver without changes or interpretation.

For instance, *without alterations*, a laboratory assistant carefully records experimental conditions and results and transmits them to his supervisor; the marketing department gathers comments from customers on a new product and transmits them to the engineering department; a project manager negotiates a budget with a general manager and communicates it to his subordinates.

- Focusing—The information is processed to enhance its function and the receiver's comprehension.

If properly implemented, the focusing mode is the most effective way of communicating, but the probability of unintentional distortion which decreases rather than enhances communicative effectiveness is significant.

A communicative system utilizing both parallel and focusing modes is schematically represented in Figure 12.1. A technical manager receives parallel communications from top management and from outside the company. Top management, for instance, communicates budget limitations, expected timing, ultimate goals. From outside the company, information is received on competitive activities, customers' needs, government regulations. The technical manager also receives a feedback by parallel flow from some subordinates. The technical manager digests this information and processes it so that it is more effectively comprehended by the project engineers. The transmittal of diversified details to the project engineer would create confusion. The selection of critical information and an appropriate emphasis are important. The project engineers further process the information received from the technical manager for the benefit of the assistants who, on a day-to-day basis, exchange information on progress with the project engineers by parallel flow. As in all effective communicative systems, a feedback loop is operative (other loops, not indicated in the illustration, create feedbacks between the technical manager, top management, and the outside).

- Confusion—The information is processed by adding non-functional details and/or omitting critical details.

When the focusing mode is improperly applied because of carelessness, lack of skill, or, occasionally, malice, confusion arises. This ineffective mode often derives from communicating from the sender's rather than the receiver's viewpoint. For instance, in the previous example, the technical manager may be advised by top management about goals, budget, and time limitations. Confusion arises if the technical manager adds to these messages an expression of concern about the ability to staff appropriately and in a timely fashion—an

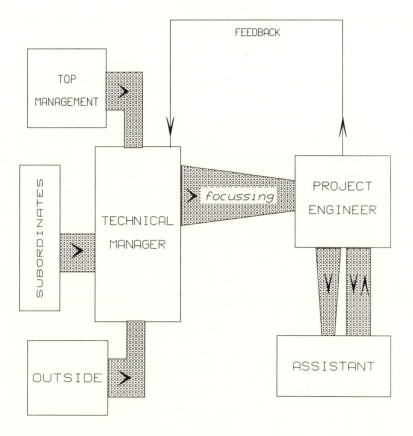

Figure 12.1 Example of a Communicative System in a New Product Development Organization

activity for which the receiver (project engineer) has no authority. Confusion also arises if critical details of the project goals are omitted.

- Logjam—The information from various sources is processed through an overloaded or ineffective person or organization.

Because information is power, the logjam mode is often intentional; hence the detection of intentional communicative bottlenecks and prompt curative action are very important. Overloaded communicative nodes constitute another source of bottlenecks and lead to substandard time management. At times, the logjam mode causes extreme negative repercussions, for instance by wasting resources for activities that should have been discontinued. Bottlenecks can also arise from lack of communicative skills. In these cases, training sessions managed internally or by a specialized consulting firms are highly desirable.

Hrand Saxenian Associates developed unique fundamentals concerning the effectiveness of communication and prescribed a simple, but powerful formula: "... express your own feelings and convictions, with consideration for the thoughts and feelings of others." After comparing an organizational communicative system to an electronic communication network, Saxenian concluded that "the criterion for judging whether any given message is signal or noise would be whether or not the message can be converted into action or decision for getting the job done."[2] A corollary follows: effective communication, as defined, can be related to effectiveness in the workplace; hence, effective communicators are likely to be superior leaders.[3]

## Information Retrieval

The generation of information is occurring at an ever-accelerating pace. Fortunately, this explosion has been paralleled by the development of rapid information retrieval systems, based on very extensive computerized files. The cure has, however, generated problems of its own, to be explained later.

New product development needs an extensive information basis, concerning, among others, technology, marketing, government regulations, international relations, and industry structure. For instance, marketing information is essential as a base for new product planning and for commercial development as described in Chapter 5. How can one satisfy these needs?

All enterprises engaged in new product development need an information resource center; most need access to one of the many computerized information retrieval systems. A simple library is no longer adequate.

To the extent possible, persons involved in the new product development process should be able, with adequate assistance, to access information directly. Ideally, both internal and external information files should be retrievable directly from each principal's desk via a computer terminal. More often, however, the principals interact through information experts staffing the resource center. In this case, the establishment of effective internal working relations is critical.

As an example, a project manager needs to assess the market segmentation of integrated circuit ceramic packaging by type, geographical areas, and end use. Several computerized files may help when descriptors and search logics are selected appropriately. Such selections must be worked out collaboratively between the project engineer and the information center expert. The narrowest possible search may be tried first, otherwise the perusal of the output may be too time consuming. The initial output may be limited to titles and later expanded selectively by retrieving abstracts and eventually copies of original documents.

Computerized information files generally are inadequate for very recent and very old information. The latter are seldom critical but the former are of paramount importance. Hence, the information center needs to maintain or have access to current periodicals which must be searched manually. Periodicals must include those that have an international character. Current periodicals have a way of finding hidden niches in individual offices, thereby negating their value to most potential users. This practice should be strongly discouraged, or duplicate copies procured.

The new product developer has alternative ways of finding information besides direct retrieval. One is to subscribe to current awareness services, or periodic newsletters. Government agencies, trade associations, and private enterprises issue such information. The problems arising from these services are many: information is always digested and the *focusing mode* may not be consistent with the readers' goals; each service covers a specialized area, hence several services may be needed, with attendant high costs; the data base on which these services depend has various degrees of thoroughness and reliability. All told, however, these services save much time and are useful, provided they are perused with a critical eye and followed up by independent retrieval of selected original information.

Government organizations are a major source of information, whose costs are generally modest. Here one of the problems is the overwhelming size of certain information files and therefore the time expended in selecting in such sources the few data that are of interest. Examples are the data from the Census of Manufactures,[4] and those concerning production and consumption of various types of energy.

Government contractors may commission searches, often at modest or no cost; all others can avail themselves of the extensive holdings of the National Technical Information Service of the U.S. Department of Commerce and acquire through that agency copies of reports.

Trade organization and professional societies are a major source of information, some of which is restricted to members. Professional societies have become publication and information centers. They often supply educational material and data bases on computer disks and videotapes as well as hard copies.

Consulting firms play a major role in information retrieval, both by way of publishing proprietary reports, and by undertaking specific searches. Some of these reports apply the parallel mode of communication; most, however, process the information input and draw conclusions from the data base. These information outputs are most valuable but must be perused with a somewhat critical eye and at times cross-examined.

## Examples

Too much of a good thing may lead to hardship. Communication is no exception. *Overcom* exemplifies the problems that may arise when information channels are very active but uncontrolled. *Stainless*, our second example, emphasizes the need to critically analyze the meaning of a marketing data base.

### Overcom

Overcom is a fictitious entrepreneurial middle-sized company very active in new product development. Its general manager, a strong believer in open communication within the company, issued a memo to his subordinates stating: "It is the policy of our company to foster free exchange of information among the members of each project team and between various organizational units." A verbal communication in a staff meeting would have afforded an opportunity for discussion and modification of this edict; but since the general manager selected an abrupt, written communication, the subordinates decided not to object. They reproduced the memo and broadcast it down the organizational lines without comments.

Project managers decided to exercise their own judgment on the extent of their compliance. They felt that overcommunication could be inefficient and possibly deleterious. Personnel at lower organizational levels did not exercise similar judgment, and, on balance, selected to be open in their relations with colleagues. Most lower-level persons communicated verbally and informally, but some felt compelled by the policy to issue written communications about many details on the status of the project, as perceived from *their* vantage points. They made copies of their memos and sent them both to subordinates and to supervisors; some of these copies were further reproduced; thus, before long, the communicative channels were cluttered by nonessential information: the confusion mode became operative.

A major problem arose when a middle-level manager received information on the status of the project from two sources: the project manager (who effectively used the focusing mode), and a subordinate, who had transmitted by memo details as perceived. The two communications were contradictory. According to the project manager, the project was essentially on track. According to the subordinate, there was a major bottleneck that appeared insurmountable. A time-consuming inquest followed, during which several team members became defensive and spent much effort to prove that they were not responsible for the bottleneck. At the end of the inquest, the bottleneck turned out to exist only in the eye of the subordinate; it was a minor snag that was promptly removed, but loomed ominous in the subordinate's mind.

Effort could have been saved and emotions avoided if the open communication policy had been interpreted appropriately at each organizational level. The subordinate would have been well advised to refrain from broadcasting nonessential details without first consulting with the supervisor; the use of verbal rather than written communication would have been, at any rate, more appropriate.

### Stainless

Marketing information on industrial materials abound, but their reliability and significance leaves much to be desired in many cases. This example focuses on the meaning of marketing information as projected from different viewpoints.

For the United States, the American Iron and Steel Institute publishes a data base comprising statistics on shipments of various stainless steel products, segmented according to end uses.[5] These statistics are very reliable, but cover only that fraction of the shipments that is sold directly to users. The balance is traded through service centers or reprocessed by intermediate fabricators such as pipe makers and rerollers. One can, however, exercise judgment on the ultimate disposition of such indirect sales, and construct a matrix whereby all shipments are segmented by type of product and by end use.

Let us analyze the meaning of that data base from different viewpoints. From the viewpoint of the companies that supply primary raw materials to stainless steel producers (e.g., ferrochrome, nickel, molybdenum), these statistics are inadequate because they do not reveal how much scrap is recycled. From the viewpoint of stainless producers who may contemplate expansions, these statistics are also wanting. They first must be supplemented with international trade data, in order to compute the apparent consumption from shipments and net trade. International trade data are readily available, but not necessarily by type of products nor by end use.

An additional problem arises when consideration is given to the international trade of components and systems containing stainless steel. If, for instance, an automotive company buying domestic stainless steels decides to import trims and exhaust systems from a foreign country, the demand for domestically produced stainless steel would decrease. The true apparent consumption, which is relatable to the economic activity of the automotive industry and the stainless steel content of each vehicle should include the stainless content of imported and exported components, but these data are difficult, if not impossible, to retrieve.

Because stainless steel is an international commodity, to restrict the marketing data base to the domestic region is inadequate for business decision making. To extend marketing research to the rest of the world is a mammoth task. The reliability of data bases, especially from some less developed countries and from the centrally planned economies, is very low; moreover, enduse segmentation, when available, may be based on applications that are different from country to country.

This example is given to emphasize that marketing data retrieved through advisory services or through published data bases must be interpreted from specific viewpoints and cross-examined.

## Conclusions

The communicative systems that are operational in new product development are similar to a telecommunication network only because they may be affected by noise and distortion. Otherwise, a telecommunication network faithfully transmits to a receiver a message as formulated by a sender. In the communicative systems operating in a complex organization, each message should be processed in order to enhance its effectiveness.

A universal rule in effective communication is to express information from the receiver's rather than the sender's viewpoint. Consideration should be given to language comprehension, goals, aspirations, and emotions of the receiver.

Nonessential details should be omitted and, more generally, overcommunication should be avoided. Verbal communications are preferred, especially in interpersonal interactions, because they give the receiver an opportunity to respond immediately. During verbal interactions, test questions should be interjected in order to ascertain whether the meaning of the messages has been comprehended.

Different media are appropriate in different circumstances. For organizational communication, electronic mail is often a preferred medium, and memoranda effective. In institutional communications mass media play an important role, but others, including judicious use of videotapes, are valuable.

In new product development, communication between technology, marketing, and manufacturing organizations are very critical. Appropriate management information systems should be set up to effect prompt and accurate communications between these units, both from the organizational and the interpersonal viewpoints. However, informal channels between individuals are very effective in the fulfillment of ultimate objectives.

Information retrieval is a special kind of communication that is vital to new product development. All enterprises engaged in these activities must have an adequate information resource center; access to computerized data base and literature search is necessary in most cases. Advisory services, proprietary reports, and customized consulting enhance information retrieval and save much time, provided that their output is critically analyzed and at times cross-examined.

Many failures can be attributed to inadequate communicative systems, but many more are caused by untimely or ineffective follow-up after critical communications are received.

## Notes

1. L. D. Thayer, *Communication and Communicative Systems in Organization, Management, and Interpersonal Relations* (Homewood, Illinois: R. D. Irwin, 1968).

2. Hrand Saxenian, "A New Prescription for Old-Fashioned Leadership," *Business Horizons* (Fall 1965): 45–53.

3. Hrand Saxenian, "To Select a Leader," *Technology Review,* 72, No. 7 (May 1970): 3–9.

4. United States Department of Commerce, Bureau of the Census, *1982 Census of Manufactures*, compiled by Berman Associates, Lanham, Maryland (Washington, DC: U.S. Government Printing Office, 1983).

5. American Iron and Steel Institute, *Shipments of Steel Products by Market Classification, Report 16-S*. Issued monthly, quarterly, and annually.

## PART V

# ROADS TO SUCCESS

# 13

---

# Three Outstanding Examples of New Product Development

## Introduction

New product development has its winners and its losers. We shall describe three disparate examples of major winners in order to emphasize that success, like failure, does not have unique origins.

The first example (*instant camera*) exemplifies the relentless effort of an individual inventor who created a revolutionary new product and a powerful enterprise. Edwin Land started with a brilliant idea and with limited resources. After achieving his original goal, he opened ever-expanding horizons in photography and satisfied countless market needs.

The second example (*anaerobic adhesives*) discussed the effort of a college professor, Vernon Krieble, who believed in the outstanding commercial potential of a new product that nobody wanted. He adapted this product to the needs of the market, and thereafter used it as a prototype for myriad other products.

The third example (*sodium bicarbonate*) shows how a very old and undifferentiated product generated sustained growth and profitability through appropriate commercial development and minimal product adaptation.

One should not surmise from these examples that prescriptions can be formulated to assure success. Each case is unique. Thus, the reader is encouraged to learn from history and to reinforce the concepts described in the preceding chapters without having the illusion that the application of such concepts assures victory. A sound methodology of new product development only increases the probability of success in this very risky area of endeavors.

## Instant Camera

### Introduction

The one-step photographic system was conceived in 1944. To understand how it was conceived and reduced to practice one should learn about the development of the first synthetic polarizing film 18 years earlier, a development that had a vital impact on the success of instant photography.

### The Synthetic Polarizing Film[1]

In 1926 Edwin Land, a Harvard student, left school shortly before graduating in order to pursue his own work. He was intrigued by an old invention—the chemical iodoquinine as a synthetic light polarizer. This invention did not achieve commercial success because the inventor failed to grow iodoquinine crystals of sufficient size. At that time polarizing screens were primarily constructed by cutting thin wafers from the natural mineral tourmaline, or by fabricating the Nicol prism from another natural mineral. The potential of light polarization, for instance to eliminate glare, was recognized, but a widespread commercialization of the existing polarizing devices was prevented by cost and raw material availability.

Land was confronted with a technical constraint—the inability to grow iodoquinine crystals larger than one-eighth of an inch. He recognized the *soft* nature of this constraint and circumvented it by conceiving a process whereby small, aligned crystals could be dispersed in a transparent medium. This conception changed the technical problem from the growth of large crystals to the alignment of small crystals. The problem was solved by applying a magnetic field to small crystals dispersed in a fluid transparent medium that was later solidified. The successful solution of this problem was then extended to other transparent media and to alternative ways of aligning the crystals. The first patent application was filed in April 1929, and covered product, processing, and uses—a broad and powerful coverage indeed.

The first commercial use of the new synthetic polarizing film occurred in 1934; the Polaroid Corporation was founded in 1937, and countless new derivative products were developed and commercialized in the ensuing eight years, helped substantially by the fulfillment of military needs during World War II. The revenues of the Polaroid Corporation grew from less than $150,000 in its first year of operation to more than 1 million dollars in 1941, and then, explosively, to nearly 17 million in 1945.

After the end of World War II revenues dropped to less than 3 million dollars, profitability vanished, and a drastic conversion from military to civilian markets became necessary. The *vector growth* based on the original polarizing film invention was no longer operative. The development of a new product became necessary to save the company from a dull and lingering existence, or possible extinction. The new product was the instant camera.

### The One-step Photographic System

At that time everybody recognized the market need for a system that allowed photographers to see the product of their work without delay. One-step photography, however, did not originate from the well-equipped laboratories of the major photographic industries, just like nylon did not originate from the textile industry. Why did the instant camera originate from a young company selling essentially a single product line—the polarizing film—that was not even essential as a component of the new product sought?

Two factors were operative. One was the courage and determination of Edwin Land, a factor that often is stronger in an entrepreneurial environment than in more stable and diversified establishments. The other factor was the accumulated technical know-how in a related area, know-how that was *transferable, given an imaginative reorientation of the ultimate focal point*. In Land's words, "... it was as if all we had done in learning to make polarizers, the knowledge of plastics and the properties of viscous liquids, the preparation of microscopic crystals smaller than the wavelength of light, the laminating of plastic sheet, living in the world of colloids in supersaturated solutions, had been a school and a preparation. ... "

The concept of the instant camera was generated in 1944 and a patent application was applied for immediately. Three years of technical development reduced the concept to practice. The first photographs could not compare in quality with those made by conventional technology. Because the density of the silver particles was low, the photographs had a sepia tone. The first camera—Model 95, the prototype of all cameras produced during the ensuing 15 years—was rather heavy and cumbersome. It took a full minute to develop the film and no negative was produced. But all these limitations were offset by the ability to see results on site. The new product was an outstanding commercial success and constituted the basis for a second explosive growth of the Polaroid Corporation.

In 1947 the new technology was demonstrated at a professional society meeting and generated enormous interest. Instantly, it made front page news on leading newspapers and magazines. In 1948 the Model 95 and the companion Type 40 film became articles of commerce. The corporation decided to have the camera manufactured by outside contractors, thus keeping its technical resources focused on chemistry and optics, rather then extending them to mechanical engineering. One year later revenues bounced back from about two and one-half to over five million dollars, 80 percent of which derived from photographic products. The polarizing film product line was retained, expanded, and partially reoriented toward civilian markets, but the photographic line remained dominant and continued to enjoy vector growth, that is, the development and marketing of a number of new products essentially derived from previously commercialized products. Corporate revenues exceeded 100 million dollars in 1961, with photographic products accounting for over 90 percent of the total. A milestone was reached in 1963 with the commercialization of color instant photography. Whereas growth continued unabated thereafter, this example will be concluded at this point in its history, after detailing how vector growth operated in the 1948–1963 period.

In that period the original product was continuously improved and adapted to many new applications and the markets expanded internationally. Just two years after the first introduction, the film was improved. Photographs were black and white, similar in appearance to conventional prints. A coater was added to improve long-term stability. The P/N film was developed, so that a negative could be instantly created. Thereafter, faster films—some exceeding the speed of conventional products—and cameras with faster lenses were developed. The processing time was reduced from 60 to 15 seconds. Application areas, and products to serve them, were expanded to radiography, press cameras, laboratory equipment, identification badges, transparencies, and others. The automatic exposure feature was added to the camera and an electric model created, with attendant development of storage batteries uniquely designed for this photographic application.

### Success Factors

The success of the Polaroid instant camera and its derivative photographic products depended very strongly on the imagination and leadership of the inventor and by outstanding technical development. Commercial development, however, played an equally important role and always proceeded simultaneously. Since the development of the first polarizing film, a policy of extensive proprietary protection was formulated and implemented. (Land has over 500 patents to his name.) The sample patent described in Chapter 10 is but one of numerous patents covering products, processing, and uses. These patents created a defensive net that was impossible to penetrate.

This strong proprietary protection allowed Polaroid Corporation to choose the timing of product introduction. Some new products were promoted immediately, others held back until the timing was most propitious, without fearing to be preempted by a competitor.

Polaroid Corporation paid much attention to product promotion and company image. It exploited television advertising as early as 1952 (remember the Dave Garroway show?). Television promotion included live network demonstrations, a very effective medium for this product line. Support to the arts, outstanding employees' benefits, and participation in government projects are only a few factors that enhanced company image.

At its fiftieth anniversary, in 1987, the Polaroid Corporation had revenues nearing two billion dollars, and product lines extending from the original polarizing films and glasses to over 150 photographic products catering to consumer, technical, and industrial end uses.

## Anaerobic Adhesives

### History[2]

The history of anaerobic adhesives parallels that of the instant camera in many respects. It occurred during the same time period. It was led initially by a single entrepreneur. It was based on the recognition of a market need. However, the entrepreneur was not the original inventor.

In 1945 a major corporation developed a new kind of adhesive, based on an organic chemical that was fluid when aerated, but set as soon as air was removed (hence the name anaerobic). Exceptional as it was, this product was difficult to market because it needed to be constantly supplied with air. One way to do this was to store it in a container attached to an air compressor. Shipping was therefore cumbersome and expensive. Hence the inventing corporation decided to drop this line.

Vernon Krieble, a chemistry professor, having heard of this invention, conceived ways of circumventing the principal technical problem (another recognition and removal of a soft constraint) by modifying the chemical so that much less air was needed to keep it fluid, and by storing it in polyethylene containers that are permeable to air. The modified product had an acceptable shelf life. Krieble then reoriented his thinking to marketing research and commercial development. One of the most obvious applications was the use of the new adhesive in lieu of lock washers—those springy components that lock nuts to bolts.

A consulting firm was hired to assess market potential and to determine the major success factors. That study reached three principal conclusions:

- There was a sizable market for thread-locking devices.
- To have appeal, the locked bolt should be reusable.
- The adhesive should be priced to be competitive with lock washers.

Whereas lock washers were very inexpensive components, the amount of the new adhesive needed in their stead was very small. Therefore the adhesive, if priced cost effectively, would generate very large margins.

Krieble and his associates circumvented the reusability problem by searching for markets in which this feature does not apply. The automotive industry appeared to be one such market, and a very large one. Commercialization was undertaken without much additional research and development.

The American Sealant Co. became operational, and promoted the new adhesive among local manufacturers, receiving a reasonable response. It later focused on the original equipment manufacturers market. Because the original product was found too strong and somewhat erratic in its performance, several modified products were developed and sold as test kits. These test kits sustained the company during its early history, generated reasonable profits, and were instrumental in obtaining valuable feedback from users.

In 1956 the new product was promoted by staging a press party when the company's revenues were only about $300 per month, and the total employment five persons. This rather bold move was crowned by success. The demand for test kits increased rapidly. In turn, feedback from satisfied users gave the company ample ammunitions for advertising based on case histories rather than on product characteristics—a much more convincing approach.

In 1963 the company changed its name to Loctite Corporation. In the intervening years, the original products were modified in order to differentiate them according to end uses. Concurrently, market targets were selected based on the best matches between product performance and market needs.

Eventually, the product line was extended by developing a new class of adhesives based on a different chemical (cyanoacrylate) which sets in the presence of moisture, rather than in the absence of air. This new line satisfied different market needs. Markets were also extended internationally, with emphasis on the Western European area.

Today the Loctite Corporation has revenues approaching a half billion dollars per year. Growth was primarily achieved from within. Acquisitions for the sole purpose of swelling revenues have been, by fundamental policy, avoided. The major products still consist of a diversified line of adhesives and sealants, based on modifications of the two original chemicals, supplemented, to a minor extent, by epoxy and acrylic products.

### Success Factors

The major success factors are based on what Loctite Corporation calls *Programmed Innovation*,[3] that is, technical developments intimately connected with knowledge of the markets and business planning. Programmed innovation implies knowledge of the business in which a company is and wants to be, where the company stands at the present, and where it wants to go in the future. It implies an intimate collaboration of technical, commercial, and business personnel, all conscious of the ever-changing environment in which they operate.

Initially, success depended on courage and determination, on a vision that escaped others, on the humility that allowed a leader to seek advice, and on the self-confidence that made the leader accept some advice while rejecting others.

This example also indicates that many ideas need only limited resources for their reduction to practice and that some new products may be very successful in one environment, while withering in another, as it happened in the case of xerography. Xerography—the dry reproduction technology—was developed with very limited resources by Chester Floyd Wilson in 1938. Major corporations were not interested in commercializing this invention, but a consulting firm convinced the Haloid Corporation, a small photo paper producer, to accept the challenge. The new product, marketed 21 years after the original invention, became the base of the corporate giant Xerox.

## Sodium Bicarbonate

### History

Baking soda—the chemical compound sodium bicarbonate—is usually associated with an upset stomach or with home baking. For some, it is associated with the registered trademark Arm and Hammer. This trademark is the property of Church & Dwight, a corporation founded in 1846, which for over a century had a single principal product and a few derivative products serving consumer, industrial, and agricultural markets. How could such a limited product portfolio sustain a company for nearly 150 years?

In 1988 Church & Dwight had revenues of about 350 million dollars with 16.5 million dollars net income. It had a respectable return on equity and an impressing domestic market share. In the 1985 to 1988 period, its revenues increased at a compound rate of nearly 15 percent per year.

This brilliant performance in an industry affected by chronic overcapacity is to a great extent the consequence of a strong new product development drive implemented since 1970. Whereas the original product—sodium bicarbonate—was adapted to new uses and derivative products developed at minimal technical effort, the dominant activities were commercial rather than technical developments. Essentially, this example emphasizes that *old products for new markets* are equivalent to new products, as far as business repercussions are concerned.

How did Church & Dwight capture these new markets? In the consumer area, the old product was adapted as a laundry detergent, and was helped in this application by the ecological concern for detergents containing phosphates. It was promoted as a deodorizer for carpets, refrigerators, and cat litter and found its way in oven cleaners, dentifrices, and bath water softeners.

In the industrial area, the old product was already extensively used by commercial bakeries. It later found its way in pharmaceuticals, fire extinguishers, and as an intermediate chemical in process industries. Of late, its use is being explored as a flue gas desulfurizer—a potentially very large market. In this application, the old product removes pollutants from flue gases without using large amounts of water. Whereas overall economics may not be favorable in certain systems, the current concerns for acid rain and for water conservation are very favorable factors in this application.

Old baking soda is also used as a cattle food supplement, because it enhances the milk output and increases the butterfat content without causing undesirable side effects.

### Success Factors

This example demonstrates that success strongly depends on a sound business plan that is implemented without vacillations, even if it deviates from more popular business approaches. It also shows that major technical developments, and especially the so-called high technology, are not a necessary ingredient for success. It indicates the power of seeking new markets for products already existing or easily derivable from other proven products, when the enterprise has strong product and company positions, and when commercial development is implemented with adequate resources and know-how.

The example also shows that societal factors—in this case, concerns for the environment—are often very important in determining the degree of commercial success of new products.

## Conclusions

These diverse examples have one common base: the need for concomitance between business planning, technical development, and commercial development in order to increase the probability of success in new product development. They are otherwise disparate, thereby demonstrating that success does not have a unique origin. They show that achievements can be found in small as well as large enterprises, in new as well as old products, in high as well as low technology. They indicate that the relentless pursuit of strong convictions is an important success factor, but that the stubborn frontal attack of certain problems may be less rewarding than the imaginative circumvention of the difficulties encountered.

### Notes

The author is indebted to Polaroid Corporation and Loctite Corporation for supplying valuable information on their histories and business philosophies.

1. Richard Saul Wurman, *Polaroid—Access—Fifty Years* (New York, New York: Access Press, Ltd., 1989).

2. Newman H. Giragosian, "Case History: Loctite Corporation—Adhesives," in *Successful Product and Business Development*, edited by N. H. Giragosian (New York: Marcel Dekker, Inc., 1978): 253–264.

3. Harry W. Coover, "Programmed Innovation—Strategy for Success," *Research Management*, 29 (December 1986): 12–17.

# 14

## Seven Guiding Lights

### Introduction

In the preceding chapters we analyzed the principal aspects of new product development—motivation, product definition, implementation mode, human side, and timing. We recommended five critical questions.

In this final chapter we shall consolidate this complex subject matter and highlight the most important facets of new product development by discussing the seven statements listed in Figure 14.1.

Readers are exhorted to continuously keep in mind those seven statements. Readers must also ask themselves related questions that specifically fit their environments and conditions. The results of these inquiries will improve the overall chance of achieving success.

### New Product Development Is a Probabilistic Phenomenon

The developers must be conscious of the probabilistic nature of their endeavors. New product development endeavors are complex, strongly dependent on diversified human resources, and significantly affected by factors and events beyond the developer's control. Thus, the belief that the implementation of a mechanical methodology can assure success is an illusion, and, at times, a delusion.

From initial generation of ideas to full commercialization, and well into the mature age of a product, the developers should strive to control what is in their power to control, and to monitor what is beyond their control.

No single facet of new product development can assure success. Few facets are so detrimental that they cannot be at least alleviated.

Because of the probabilistic nature of new product development, planning and assessments must consider *long-term* repercussions.

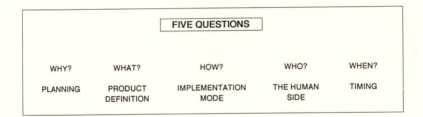

FIVE QUESTIONS

| WHY? | WHAT? | HOW? | WHO? | WHEN? |
|------|-------|------|------|-------|
| PLANNING | PRODUCT DEFINITION | IMPLEMENTATION MODE | THE HUMAN SIDE | TIMING |

SEVEN STATEMENTS

NEW PRODUCT DEVELOPMENT IS A PROBABILISTIC PHENOMENON

NEW PRODUCT DEVELOPMENT IS AN INTERFUNCTIONAL PROCESS

MOST FOUNDATIONS OF NEW PRODUCT DEVELOPMENT ARE SUBJECTIVE

EACH NEW PRODUCT DEPENDS ON THE ENTIRE PORTFOLIO

COMPETITION MUST BE BROADLY DEFINED

INTELLECTUAL PROPERTY MUST BE PROTECTED

NEW PRODUCT DEVELOPMENT CAPABILITIES MUST BE REGENERATED

Figure 14.1  Summary of the New Product Development Process Described in Terms of Five Questions and Seven Statements

## New Product Development Is an Interfunctional Process

*Interfunctional* signifies that no organizational sector—technology, marketing, finance, manufacturing—can, in isolation, effectively plan and implement new product development. *Process* signifies that new product development needs resources and generates an output through a series of dynamic actions.

Business planning, technology, and marketing must be integrated at all stages of the process, and top management must see to it that such integration is effective.

Because the process is dynamic, developers must be sensitive to the value of time. Time is critical because of the time value of money, and because certain opportunities have limited time windows. A product may reach the market too late and reap only mild benefits. A product may be premature and gain little acceptance during the most critical phase of its life.

The dynamic nature of the process demands that assessment be carried out repeatedly, considering changes that have occurred both within and outside the organization. Planning should be revised accordingly.

## Most Foundations of New Product Development Are Subjective

In new product development, few indicators, including most market research data, can be measured objectively. The unavoidable biases and uncertainties must be alleviated by considering a variety of viewpoints, and making assessments by consensus. The combined opinion of insiders and outsiders is especially effective in removing biases and reaching mature judgment.

Assessments implemented by a diversified group of people are much more meaningful if the group first agrees on the criteria on which such assessments will be based.

## Each New Product Depends on the Entire Portfolio

Many new products affect the marketability of preexisting products. In addition, all new products affect, directly or indirectly, the management of the rest of the product portfolio.

From the financial viewpoint, there must be a balance between products that are cash generators and products that need cash for their growth. From the marketing viewpoint, there may be synergistic effects that improve the company position or competitive effects that weaken it. From the manufacturing viewpoint, new products may improve the utilization of installed facilities or require major investments.

The portfolio, including commercial and developmental products, must be reviewed periodically.

## Competition Must Be Broadly Defined

The analysis of competitors must consider all geographical areas that affect the manufacturing and marketing of the product. The internal structure and the distribution channels of the competing manufacturers must be understood.

The assessment of competing products should not be limited to those products that compete directly. Consideration should be given to all products that fulfill the same functions for the benefit of the customers.

## Intellectual Property Must Be Protected

The know-how that makes a new product possible is legally defined as an intellectual property. Such property must be considered as an asset, albeit intangible.

In addition to specific know-how, the organizations that develop new products have data and knowledge, partially recorded in documents or data bases, and partially embedded in the minds of their employees and advisors. All these assets must be protected.

Some intellectual property is protectable according to the statutes of various countries; hence patents, copyright, and trademarks can be obtained. Other intellectual property can be kept secret and should be readily retrievable.

Personnel engaged in new product development must, at all times, be sensitive to the proprietary protection issues and to the need for keeping appropriate records.

## New Product Development Capabilities Must Be Regenerated

A capability is defined as the totality of human, physical, and informational resources that make an organization capable of achieving a given goal—in this case, the development of successful new products.

Manufacturing and marketing capabilities normally expand as a business enterprise achieves success, and are curtailed in case of failures. A peculiar characteristic of new product development capabilities is that they are often impaired not only by failures, but also by successes.

After failures, new product development organizations are often disbanded or severely reduced. After successes, human resources are often redeployed because of promotional opportunities in other sectors, physical facilities either decommissioned or absorbed into manufacturing plants, informational files relegated to dead storage.

Investing in the regeneration of new product development capabilities pays handsome dividends.

## Conclusions

The five questions recommended at the beginning of this book established a disciplined approach to the new product development process. The seven statements explained in this concluding chapter recapitulated what must be kept in mind at all times.

In new product development failure is the norm; success, the exception. The integration of various disciplines and human resources is critical; relentless and effective leadership, essential.

Ultimately, courage and determination are the main ingredients along the roads to success.

# Bibliography

American Iron and Steel Institute. *Shipments of Steel Products by Market Classification, Report 16-S.* Issued monthly, quarterly, and annually.

Bell Telephone Laboratories. *Authorization for Work—Solid State Physics—The Fundamental Investigation of Conductors, Semiconductors, Insulators, Piezoelectric and Magnetic Materials,* July 1945.

Burek, Deborah M., Koek, Karin E., and Novallo, Annette. *Encyclopedia of Associations® 1990.* Detroit, MI: Gale Research Inc., 1989.

Cady, John F., and Buzzell, Richard D. *Strategic Marketing.* Boston, MA: Little, Brown & Company, 1986.

Coover, Harry W. "Programmed Innovation—Strategy for Success." *Research Management* 29 (December 1986): 12–17

Dun's Marketing Services, Inc. *Dun's Consultant Directory® 1989.* Parsippany, NJ: Dun's Marketing Services, Inc., 1988.

√ Flesher, Dale L., and Flesher, T. K. *The New Product Decision.* Montvale, NJ: National Association of Accounters, 1984.

General Electric Company. *GE R&D. The First Seventy-Five Years.* Schenectady, NY: General Electric Company, 1975.

Giragosian, Newman H. "Case History: Loctite Corporation—Adhesives." In *Successful Product and Business Development,* edited by N. H. Giragosian. New York: Marcel Dekker, Inc., 1978, pp. 253–264.

Giragosian, Newman H. "Case History: E. I. Du Pont de Nemours & Co.—Corfam." In *Successful Product and Business Development,* edited by N. H. Giragosian. New York: Marcel Dekker, 1978, pp. 264–274.

Glasser, Alan. *Research and Development Management.* Englewood Cliffs, NJ: Prentice-Hall, Inc., 1982.

Haggerty, James J. *Spinoff 1988.* National Aeronautics and Space Administration, Office of Commercial Programs Technology Utilization Division. Washington, DC: U.S. Government Printing Office, August 1988.

Hanson, W. T., Jr. "Research at Kodak." *The British Journal of Photography* 116 (3 January 1969): 8–11, 13.

Integrated Circuit Engineering Corporation. *Status 1989. A Report on the Integrated Circuit Industry.* Scottsdale, AZ: Integrated Circuit Engineering Corporation, 1989. Published yearly.

Kotler, Philip, Consulting Author. *The Military Metaphor.* 3/4" U-matic Format Videotape, Part of a Series Entitled "The Great Marketing Wars." Produced by Burton Kaplan Company, 1984. Distributed by Prentice Hall.

Mardon, J., and Mardon, L. D. *Principles and Details Mechanics of Research Direction and Management*. Gardenvale, Quebec, Canada: National Business Publications Ltd., 1968.

McKenna, Regis. *The Regis Touch. Million-dollar Advice from America's Top Marketing Consultant*. Reading, MA: Addison-Wesley Publishing Co., Inc., 1985.

Mees, C. E. Kenneth. *The Organization of Industrial Scientific Research*. 1st Edition. New York: McGraw-Hill Book Company, 1920.

Middendorf, W. H. *What Every Engineer Should Know About Inventing*. New York: Marcel Dekker, 1981.

Miller, Jule A. *From Ideas to Profit*. New York: Van Nos Reinhold, Division of International Thompson Publishing Corp., 1986.

*Million Dollar Directory®. America's Leading Public and Private Companies*. Parsippany, NJ: The Dun & Bradstreet Corporation, 1989.

Nicolet Instrument Corporation, "A Comprehensive Instrument for Clinical Audiology and Hearing Aid Fitting." *Hearing Instruments* 38, no. 1 (1987): 37–38, 64.

Porter, Michael E. *Competitive Strategy—Techniques for Analyzing Industries and Competitors*. New York: The Free Press, a Division of Macmillan Publishing Co., Inc., 1980.

Prince, George M. "Synectics®: Twenty-Five Years of Research into Creativity and Group Process." *Training and Development Journal* 201 (1982): 76–79.

Reeves, E. Duer. *The Management of Industrial Research*. New York: Reinhold Publishing Corporation, 1967.

Roeser, Ross J., and Taylor, Kenya. "Audiometric and Field Testing with a Digital Hearing Instrument." *Hearing Instruments* 39, no.4 (1988): 14–16, 18, 20, 22.

Rosenau, Milton D., Jr. *Innovation. Managing the Development of Profitable New Products*. Belmont, CA: Lifetime Learning Publications, a Division of Wadsworth, Inc., 1982.

Samuels, Jeffrey M., Ed. *Patent, Trademark and Copyright Law*. 1985 Edition. Washington, DC: The Bureau of National Affairs, Inc., 1985.

Saxenian, Hrand. "A New Prescription for Old-Fashioned Leadership." *Business Horizons* (Fall 1965): 45–53.

Saxenian, Hrand. "To Select a Leader." *Technology Review* 72, no. 7 (May 1970): 3–9.

Servi, I. S. "Information Transfer—Handle with Care." *Research Management* 19 (1976): 10–14.

Servi, I. S., and Jaffee, R. I. "Metals Requirements of the Electric Power Industry." *Materials and Society* 10, no.3 (1986): 329–343.

Sharrard, George F. "Understanding the Environment of New Business Ventures." In *Successful Product and Business Development*, edited by N. H. Giragosian. New York: Marcel Dekker, 1978, p. 102.

Sheridan, J. H. "Matrix Maze. Are two bosses better than one?" *Industry Week* 201 (June 11, 1979): 76–79.

Souder, William E. *Managing New Product Innovations*. Lexington, MA: D. C. Heath and Company Lexington Books, a Raytheon Company, 1987.

*Standard & Poor's Register of Corporations, Directors, and Executives*. New York: Standard & Poor's Corporation, a McGraw-Hill Financial Service Company, 1989.

Technology Innovation Program, *Program Solicitation.* Tyson's Corner, VA: Advanced Technology Innovations, Inc. Issued periodically

Thayer, L. D. *Communication and Communicative Systems in Organization, Management, and Interpersonal Relations.* Homewood, IL: R. D. Irwin, 1968.

"The Thinking Man's CEO." *Inc.* 10, no. 11 (November 1988): 22–34.

*United States Constitution,* Bill of Rights, Article 1, Section 8.

United States, Department of Commerce, Bureau of the Census. *1982 Census of Manufactures.* Compiled by Berman Associates, Lanham, MD. Washington, DC: U.S. Government Printing Office, 1983.

United States, Department of Commerce, Bureau of the Census. *Current Industrial Reports.* Published periodically.

United States, Department of Commerce, International Trade Administration. *1989 U.S. Industrial Outlook. Prospects for over 350 Industries.* Washington, DC: U.S. Government Printing Office, 1989. Published yearly.

United States, Department of Commerce, Patent and Trademark Office. *Basic Facts about Trademarks.* Revised. Washington, DC: U.S. Government Printing Office, August 1988.

United States, Department of the Interior, Bureau of Mines. *Minerals Yearbook, Volume I.* Washington, DC: U.S. Government Printing Office. Published yearly.

United States, Executive Office of the President, Office of Management and Budget. *Standard Industrial Classification Manual.* Washington, DC: U.S. Government Printing Office, 1987.

United States, Federal Technology Transfer Act of 1986. Public Law 99-502, October 20, 1986.

United States, Library of Congress, Copyright Office, *Copyright Basics,* Circular 1. Washington, DC: U.S. Government Printing Office, 1988.

United States, Small Business Administration, Office of Innovation Research and Technology, Washington, DC. *Pre-Solicitation Announcements.* Issued periodically.

Von Hippel, E. "Get New Products from Customers." *Harvard Business Review* 60 (1982): 117–122.

Wallenstein, Gerd D. *Concept & Practice of Product Planning.* New York: American Management Association, Inc., 1968.

*Ward's Business Directory of Major International Companies™.* Belmont, CA: Information Access Company, Division of Ziff Davis Publishing Co., 1988.

Webster, Frederick E., Jr. *Industrial Marketing Strategies.* 2nd Edition. New York: John Wiley & Sons, 1984.

Wensberg, Peter C. *Land's Polaroid. A Company and the Man Who Invented it.* Boston, MA: Houghton Mifflin Co., 1987.

Wind, Yoram, and Mahajan, Vijay. "Designing Product and Business Portfolios." *Harvard Business Review* 59 (1981): 155–165.

Wurman, Richard Saul. *Polaroid—Access—Fifty Years.* New York: Access Press, Ltd., 1989.

# Index

# About the Author

ITALO S. SERVI is a consultant to the Boston consulting firm Charles River Associates Incorporated and an adjunct faculty member at Northeastern University.

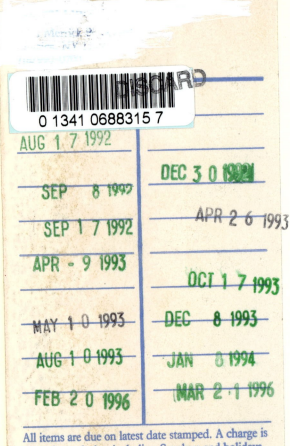